Stories to Play With

Stories to Play With

Kids' Tales Told with Puppets, Paper, Toys, and Imagination

Hiroko Fujita
Adapted & Edited by Fran Stallings

August House Publishers, Inc.
LITTLE ROCK

Originally published in Japanese in 1996 by Isseisha,
under the title of *Ohanashi Obasan No Kodougu* written by Hiroko Fujita
Copyright © 1996 Hiroko Fujita
Illustrations by Kyoko Kobayashi
with photos by Kishimoto Masayoshi and Kishimoto Masato
English translation rights arranged with Isseisha through Japan Foreign-Rights Center

English version adapted and edited by Fran Stallings,
with permission of Hiroko Fujita and Isseisha Publishing Company.
Translations by Mitsuko Harada and Satomi Obata.
Additional illustrations by Hiroko Fujita and Fran Stallings.

Published 1999 by August House, Inc.,
P.O. Box 3223, Little Rock, Arkansas, 72203, 501-372-5450
Printed in the United States of America

2 4 6 8 10 9 7 5 3

LIBRARY OF CONGRESS CATALOGING-IN-PUBLICATION DATA
Fujita, Hiroko, 1937–
　　[Ohanashi obasan no dōgu. English]
　　Stories to play with : kids' tales told with puppets, paper, toys, and
imagination / by Hiroko Fujita ; adapted & edited by Fran Stallings ;
illustrated by Kyoko Kobayashi, Hiroko Fujita, and Fran Stallings ;
[translations by Mitsuko Harada and Satomi Obata].
　　　　p.　　cm.
　　ISBN 0-87483-553-4 (trade paper : alk. paper)
　　1. Storytelling. 2. Activity programs in education. 3. Play.
I. Stallings, Fran. II. Title.
LB1042.F84 1999　　　　　　　　　　　　　　　　99-12427

Executive editor: Liz Parkhurst
Project Editor: Jason H. Maynard
Cover Design: Harvill Ross Studios Ltd.
Layout: Ira and Carron Hocut

AUGUST HOUSE, INC.　　PUBLISHERS　　LITTLE ROCK

For the children of
Japan and America
who helped us to develop
these stories.

Contents

Pronunciation Guide

In Japanese words, please pronounce vowels

a as in "father"
e as in "pet"
i as in "ski"
o as in "so"
u as in "rhubarb"

The biggest difference is in stress patterns. Rapid American English often stresses one syllable in a long word or phrase, and then mashes the other syllables together: "What are you doing?" can become "Cha DOON?" Even when Japanese folks talk fast, they still enunciate <u>very</u> crisply. Every syllable gets equal time and almost equal stress. In most words the tones don't go up and down, but tick off with metronomic regularity.

Thus, *botamochi* is not *BOtaMOchi* but *bo-ta-mo-chi*. Doubled vowels get equal time: *juubako* has four beats *(ju-u-ba-ko)*.

The chant, *"Haa, sono tori,"* has the following 4/4 rhythm:

HA . a . | SO no to . | RI . . .

Preface

Maybe you feel that it is hard to tell a story.

But while little children are drawing on scrap paper, or zooming a toy car around, they say to themselves, "Brrm, brrm, this is the bus to the amusement park—everybody in! Brrm, brrm, are you going to get in, Mrs. Bear? Brrm, brrm, you too, Mr. Pig? Brrm, brrm, it may be a bumpy ride..."

That, I think, is the start of storytelling. It may be hard to start from nothing, but when you have a pencil, a little car, some object or other, the world of story will spread out from there.

Let's imitate the way children do it.

First, let's tell a story using the toys we are usually wearing — our fingers. A thumb looks like a person; a fist looks like a house. All it takes is imagination.

With the help of imagination, we can tell a story while folding a sheet of newspaper or a handkerchief.

A story about a dandelion would be nicest in a field where they are actually in bloom. But if you make a dandelion from origami paper or felt, you can tell the dandelion story anywhere.

If you open a milk carton and color it, you can make a puppet of the story's hero.

You can make a village of animals out of tissue boxes side by side, with animal faces on them.

Some of my stories are based on ideas I got from the children, like the dandelion story in this book. Some are based on children's songs like "Doggie Policeman," which you can readily turn into puppet plays.

The stories in this book are just to get you started.

Please go on to make up your own stories!

— *Hiroko Fujita*

Uses For This Book

When Fujita-san first wrote this book in Japan, she was just trying to provide a basic handbook for beginners who wanted to share stories with small children. But as soon as our home-published English draft got into the hands of American adults and children alike, new uses began to appear.

As expected, educators, librarians, and youth workers took encouragement from Fujita-san's urging to "play" the story. Folks who had never dared tell without a book before, shared their delight in the toys and props with young children whose demand to "Tell it again!" soon had the little ones telling along with the adult. The craft ideas and activities have been used in schools and libraries, camps and Sunday schools, home-schools and daycares.

Hearing-impaired: Teachers and librarians working with deaf children immediately saw that these stories' visual aids and simple language make them readily adaptable for students who can't hear all the words. "I usually have to rewrite stories to tell," said Sue Galloway, media specialist at the Oklahoma State School for the Deaf, "but these are ready to use." Children at St. Joseph's School for the Deaf in New York City took their toys home and retold the stories to their delighted parents.

English as a Second Language (ESL), Foreign Language Instruction: As Lima, OH, ESL instructor Sandra Liechty first pointed out to us, students can follow these stories without knowing any of the English words; but on subsequent hearings, particularly when they begin to chant along, they pick up the words in a memorable and meaningful context. Similarly, foreign language instructors like Christine Pryor, elementary school Spanish instructor in Edmond, OK, are teaching vocabulary through increasingly bilingual tellings of these stories. They easily introduce animal names and sounds, terms for family members, nouns and verbs, with visual reinforcement from the props and gestures. Eventually, students can retell the whole story in another language!

Japanese culture: The last three tales in the book, coming from the heart of Japan's traditional countryside, have obvious application in Social Studies units. Less obvious are the stories adapted from Japanese folk tradition and children's lore (see Story Sources, page 91). The illustrations in this book have not been Americanized, with the exception of the policeman and masked burglar in "Burglar's Hideout." In "Handkerchief Story," notice Mama's slippers (Japanese people never wear street shoes indoors) and Grandma's kimono. Some Japanese writing has been left in the illustrations: for instance, sounds made by people and cows in "Mr Brown. and Mr. Black," page 15, by the storyteller in "Squeak Squeak Squeak," and by the sinking boat in "Rain Hat." Can you find more?

Student storytellers: We were surprised and delighted when older children took off with this book, saying "I can do that!" At first intrigued by the origami and craft diagrams, they quickly sought younger listeners: "Here, let me show you something." And thus the stories went back into folk tradition, transmitted from child to child.

Upper elementary, middle school, and high school students reap enormous benefits from learning to share stories with younger listeners. Verbal fluency, poise, self-esteem, and community building between age groups are just a few of the benefits cited to us by educators and youth workers. We are proud that the book is being used to encourage this kind of growth.

Fran now uses the book in her school residencies nationwide and overseas, teaching story retelling skills to students from second grade to high school. Even tough alternative high school students, preparing to visit neighborhood Headstart youngsters, took to these tales and crafts with glee. "It gave them a chance to play again," noted one counselor.

Hiroko Fujita wrote this handbook to fill a gap in Japan: there were no "How To" manuals for novice storytellers working with young children. Although Americans and Canadians have many storytelling manuals, we hope this one offers a special playful approach which will encourage many more people to discover the joy of storytelling. Please feel free to tell these tales in face-to-face settings, and by all means add your own embellishments! (For permission to copy, reprint or record these stories, please contact Fran Stallings, care of August House; P.O. Box 3223; Little Rock Arkansas, 72203.)

— *Fran Stallings*

This Is How
We Begin

Which Side Won?

Let the fingers of your right hand and left hand stand up in order, starting with the thumb, to compete in laughing and talking contests.

You can do all the roles with both your hands, or you can ask some children to do the right hand and others to do the left, so that many children can enjoy participating.

Right Hand Father and Left Hand Father had a contest.

> *Hold up thumbs.*

What kind of contest was it?
A laughing contest!

WA HA HA HA, YA HA HA HA
WO HO HO HO, YO HO HO HO
    WA HA HA HA, YA HA HA HA
    WO HO HO HO, YO HO HO HO

Well, which side won?

Right Hand Mother and Left Hand Mother had a contest.

> *Hold up index fingers.*

What kind of contest was it?
A talking contest!

> *(Make up talk about weather, brag about children, nag about chores, etc.)*

Well, which side won?

Right Hand Big Brother and Left Hand Big Brother had a contest.

> *Hold up middle fingers.*

What kind of contest was it?
A hollering contest!

NYAH NYAH NA NYAH NYAH
    NYAH NYAH NA NYAH NYAH

Well, which side won?

Right Hand Big Sister and Left Hand Big Sister had a contest.

> *Hold up ring fingers.*

What kind of contest was it?
A quiet contest!
....
    ....
Well, which side won?

Right Hand Baby and Left Hand Baby had a contest.

> *Hold up pinky fingers.*

What kind of contest was it?
A crying contest!

WAH WAH BOO HOO HOO
    WAH WAH BOO HOO HOO

Well, which side won?

Mr. Brown & Mr. Black

Tell the story while making four different positions with each hand.

1. This is Mr. Brown

Right hand — A

2. This is Mr. Black

Left hand — A

3. This is Mr. Brown's house.

Right hand — B

4. This is Mr. Black's house.

Left hand — B

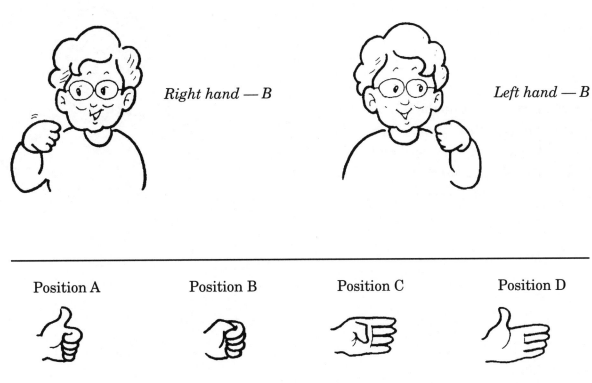

Position A   Position B   Position C   Position D

5. Mr Brown and Mr. Black are very good friends. One morning they woke up, each in his own house.

Jostle both hands, position B

6. Mr. Brown opened his door.
Right hand — C

7. He came outside.
Right hand — D

8. He closed his door.
Right hand — A

9. Mr. Brown went up the hill and down the hill to Mr. Black's house for a visit.
Right hand — A, left hand — B
Travel right hand up and down towards left fist.

10. Mr. Brown knocked on Mr. Black's door.
   Tap right thumb against left fist

He knocked and knocked, but there was no answer.

11. So Mr. Brown went back home, up the hill and down the hill.
   Travel right hand — A
   up & down away from left hand — B.

12. Mr. Brown opened his door.
   Right hand — D

13. He went inside.
   Right hand — C

14. He closed his door.
   Right hand — B

Now you have two closed fists — B

15. Mr. Black opened his door.
    Left hand—C

16. He came outside.
    Left hand — D

17. He closed his door.
    Left hand — A

18. Mr. Black went up the hill and down the hill to Mr. Brown's house for a visit.
    Left hand — A, right hand — B
    Travel left hand up and down
    towards right fist.

19. Mr. Black knocked on Mr. Brown's door.
    Tap left thumb against right fist

He knocked and knocked, but there was no answer.

20. So Mr. Black went back home, up the hill and down the hill.
    Travel left hand — A up & down
    away from right hand — B.

21. Mr. Black opened his door.
    Left hand — D

22. He went inside.
    Left hand — C

23. He closed his door.
    Left hand — B

Again you have two closed fists — B

24. Then they <u>both</u> opened their doors.
    Both hands — C

25. They both came out.
    Both hands — D

26. They both closed their doors.
    Both hands — A

27. They both went up the hill and down the hill to each other's houses, but —
    Travel hands — A up & down
    towards each other

28. They met in the middle!
    Jostle both hands — A — together

They were very happy to see each other. They had a good visit.

29. Then it was time to go home. Bye bye!
    Wave hands — A — up and down

30. They each went back, up the hill and down the hill.
    *Both hands — A — move apart,
    then up and down*

31. They each opened their doors.
    Both hands — D

32. They each went inside.
    Both hands — C

33. They each closed their doors.
    Both hands — B

34. Good night, Mr. Brown and Mr. Black!
    Nod with right, left fists — B

Comment

I learned this story from an American, so the characters are named Mr. Black and Mr. Brown. But you can change their names to anything you like, perhaps people the children know, to make the story more interesting.

And you can create a conversation for the two friends when they meet on the hill. For instance:

"Oh, Mr. Jacobs (a teacher), hello!"

"Ms. Washington (their principal), hello!"

"How are things going?"

"Oh, Josh learned how to jump rope."

"Yes, I saw him jumping!"

"And today, Kyla pushed Miki on the swings."

"Oh, that is so nice."

Ms. Fox

This can be an active children's game, or a story presented with glove puppets.

Children   Beyond the mountain,
             beyond the river.
             Ms. Fox, are you there?
Fox   Yes, I am.
Children   What are you doing?
Fox   I have just gotten up.
Children   Hah, you are a lazy bones!

Children   Beyond the mountain,
             beyond the river.
             Ms. Fox, are you there?
Fox   Yes, I am.
Children   What are you doing?
Fox   I'm in the bathroom.
Children   Hah, what a smell!

Children   Beyond the mountain,
             beyond the river.
             Ms. Fox, are you there?
Fox   Yes, I am.
Children   What are you doing?
Fox   I am putting on my makeup.
Children   Hah, what a fashion model!

Children   Beyond the mountain,
             beyond the river.
             Ms. Fox, are you there?
Fox   Yes, I am.
Children   What are you doing?
Fox   I am licking my lips.
Children   Hah, you are greedy.

Children   Beyond the mountain,
             beyond the river.
             Ms. Fox, are you there?
Fox   Yes, I am.
Children   What are you doing?
Fox   I am eating breakfast.
Children   What are you having
             for breakfast?
Fox   Snakes and frogs.
Children   Are they still alive, or
             already dead?
Fox   *Alive!*
Children   Yow, we are scared!

Comment

To play this as an active game, one child playing the role of Ms. Fox hides behind something (tree, desk, door frame).

The other children chant a dialogue with Ms. Fox. Each time they say, "Beyond the mountain, beyond the river...," they come a little closer to Ms. Fox's hiding place.

On the line *"Alive!"* Ms. Fox jumps out and chases the children back to their original position as they scream "Yow, we are scared!"

Ms. Fox catches one of the children, and that child takes the role of Ms. Fox next time.

How To:

Material: 2 cotton work gloves, one orange, one skin tone.
felt scraps of many colors
black beads (for eyes), red thread.
stuffing
Tools: scissors, thread, needle, glue.

Ms. Fox: Put the orange glove on your left hand. Hold up your index and baby fingers (fox's ears), put thumb, middle and ring fingers together (fox's snout).

Children:

1. Stuff finger tips of skintone glove for heads.
2. Draw up a line of gathering stitches to make each neck.
3. Make clothing from felt scraps. <u>With glove on</u>, wrap & glue clothes in place around your fingers.
4. Sew black bead eyes and red thread mouth onto each fingertip face.
5. Make hair from felt and glue it on the heads. BOY hair is cute if you leave some sticking out. Glue GIRL hair on front first, then back, then sides.

Children

glove puppet
on right hand

Ms. Fox

plain glove
on left hand

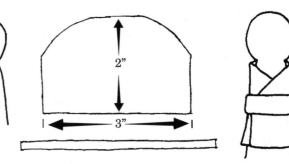

2"

3"

boy

1"

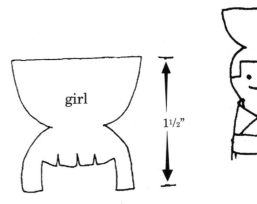

girl

1½"

A Mysterious House

You make a two-floor house from a milk carton and tell the story while you are opening each window. Let the children try to figure out the mystery.

1. This house has two floors.
   Show AB side. Point to top window on B.

I wonder who lives at this window on the second floor? I'll visit there.

TAP TAP
Sound of knocking on the window

Who lives in this room? Oh, it's you, Mr. Fox. Hello, Mr. Fox.

That was Mr. Fox's room.

2. Well, I wonder who lives at this window on the first floor?
   Point to bottom window on A

TAP TAP

Who lives in this room? Oh! It's you, Ms. Raccoon. Hello, Ms. Raccoon.

That was Ms. Raccoon's room.

View 1 Mr. Fox   *View 2* Ms. Raccoon

3.   *Slip to BC side.*
   Point to top window on B side

Remember who lives in this room? It's Mr. Fox, isn't it? Isn't that right? So I will open the window.

Well, it's Mr. Pig! That's strange, isn't it?

4.   *Turn over = sides DA*
   Point to bottom window on A

Remember who lives in this room? It's Ms. Raccoon, isn't it? Right? So I will open the window.

Well, it's Ms. Cat! That's strange, isn't it?

View 3 Mr. Pig   *View 4* Ms. Cat

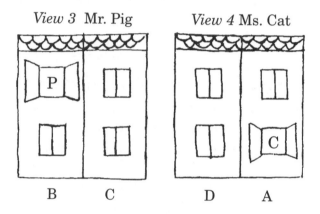

5.   *Slip the sides again*

Well, I wonder who is in this window?
   Let children guess.

Oh, how strange! (or, Yes, you are right!)

6.   *Slip or flip the sides again*

Do you remember who was living in this room? Well?

7. This is a mysterious house which changes each time I open a window.
   Isn't that strange?

How To:

Material: one milk carton (1qt), white paper, colored paper.

Tools: scissors, paste, knife for cutting.

1. Cut off top and bottom of carton.
2. Glue on colored paper for the roof.
3. Glue on white paper for the walls.
4. Draw eight windows, two on each side as shown.
5. Cut open <u>only</u> the first floor window on the A side and the second floor window on the B side. Cut on **heavy** lines only.
6. Stick the animal pictures to the inside surface of the uncut windows, as shown.
7. When you show it to the children, flatten the house so that only sides AB, BC or DA show, and open one window.

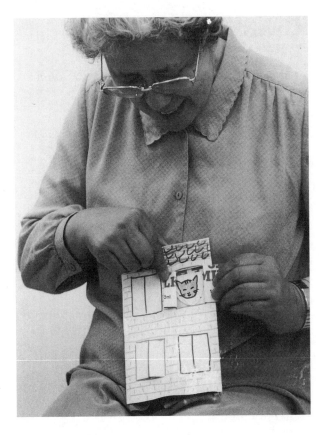

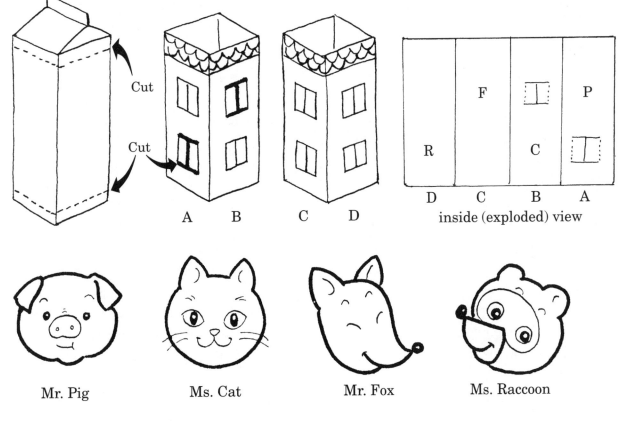

inside (exploded) view

Mr. Pig   Ms. Cat   Mr. Fox   Ms. Raccoon

Crab's Persimmons

You tell the story while turning the pages of the little book.

1. This is a crab.
2. The crab found a persimmon seed.
3. The crab planted the seed.
4. The crab watered it and said, "Sprout quickly, or I'll dig you up with my claws!"
5. The seed sprouted. The crab watered it and said, "Grow up quickly, or I'll nip you with my claws!"
6. The sprout grew. The crab said, "Grow up more quickly, or I'll nip you with my claws!"
7. The tree grew bigger. The crab said, "Bear plenty of fruit quckly, or I'll nip you with my claws!"
8. The tree bore plenty of fruit. The crab said, "Get ripe quickly, or I'll nip you with my claws!"
9. The fruit ripened. But crabs can't climb trees, so the crab didn't get any persimmons.

At the end, unfold the book and show the big picture on the back of the paper.

How To:

Material: one sheet of paper
Tools: crayons or markers, scissors

Fold the paper into 8 rectangles:
- - - - - - - - - "valley fold" (crease inside)
— • — • — • — "mountain fold" (crease up)
Number rectangles and draw in the pictures.

CUT on the heavy line, then fold up the little book as shown below.

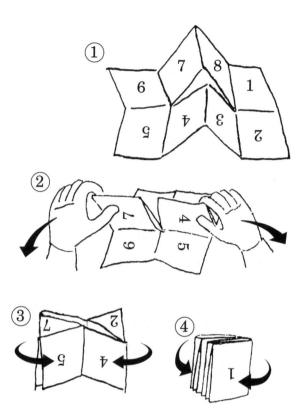

Comment

This little book can be used to help children retell any story which is divisible into 8 or 9 scenes, such as "This is the House that Jack Built" (8 parts: Jack, house, malt, rat, cat, dog, cow, maiden) or "The Gingerbread Man" (gingerbread man, grandpa, grandma, cow, pig, dog, cat, fox).

It can also be used for endless loop stories like "The Only Thing I'm Afraid Of Is —" (pg 62). Just keep turning over the pages!

Front:

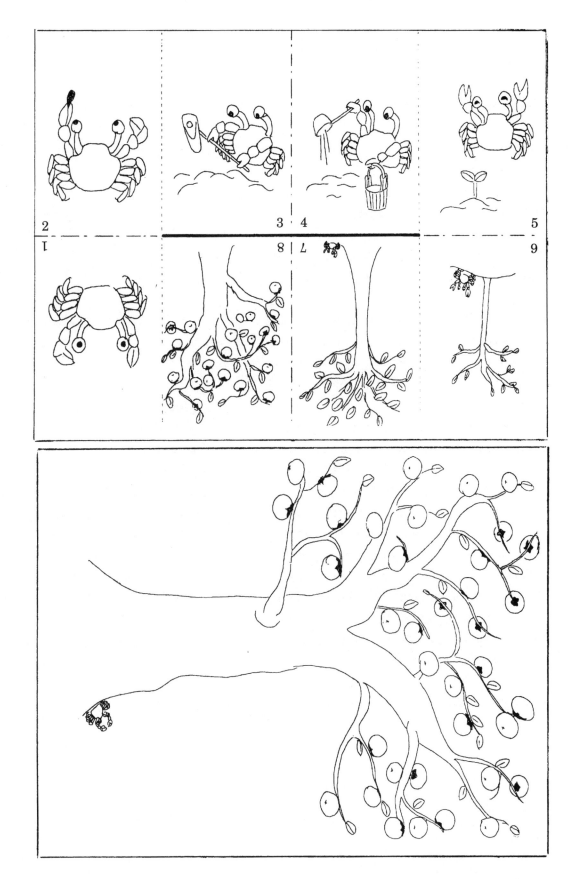

Back:

Squeak!
Squeak!
Squeak!

You can do this fingerplay with or without the puppets. Keep extra puppets "in the nest" (behind your back), using your other hand to put them on and off. Children can accompany you with their bare fingers.

Squeak squeak squeak, one mouse squeaks,
  Goes to the nest, and — two mice squeak!
Squeak squeak squeak, two mice squeak,
  Go to the nest, and — three mice squeak!
Squeak squeak squeak, three mice squeak,
  Go to the nest, and — four mice squeak!
Squeak squeak squeak, four mice squeak,
  Go to the nest, and — five mice squeak!

Squeak squeak squeak, five mice squeak,
  Go to the nest, and — four mice squeak!
Squeak squeak squeak, four mice squeak,
  Go to the nest, and — three mice squeak!
Squeak squeak squeak, three mice squeak,
  Go to the nest, and — two mice squeak!
Squeak squeak squeak, two mice squeak,
  Go to the nest, and — one mouse squeaks!
Squeak squeak squeak, one mouse squeaks,
Goes to the nest, and — say goodbye!

Finger Play Actions:

Wave your raised hand, with extended index finger (first mouse), in time to the first line. "Goes to the nest": put this hand behind your back. When you bring it back out, TWO fingers (index and middle) are extended. Wave in time to the words.

Add another finger for each mouse, finally the thumb for the fifth mouse: 1, 2, 3, 4, 5.

Then repeat, this time decreasing one finger in each verse: 5, 4, 3, 2, 1.

After the last one "goes to the nest," show an open empty palm and then wave. "Say goodbye!"

How To:

Material: felt scraps (pink for ears)
stuffing
black beads for eyes
Tools: needle, thread, scissors

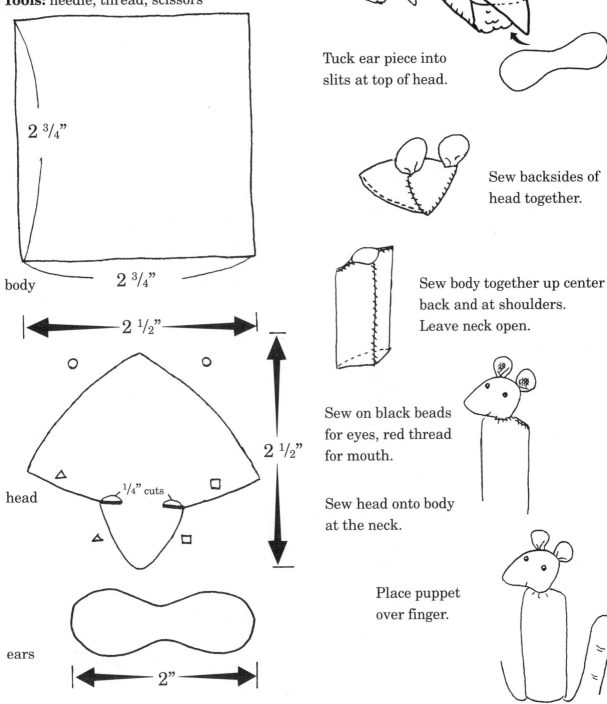

body $2\frac{3}{4}$" $2\frac{3}{4}$"

head $2\frac{1}{2}$" $2\frac{1}{2}$" $\frac{1}{4}$" cuts

ears   2"

Sew undersides of head together under chin. Stuff.

Tuck ear piece into slits at top of head.

Sew backsides of head together.

Sew body together up center back and at shoulders. Leave neck open.

Sew on black beads for eyes, red thread for mouth.

Sew head onto body at the neck.

Place puppet over finger.

Origami Mice

NOTE: these diagrams zigzag down the page

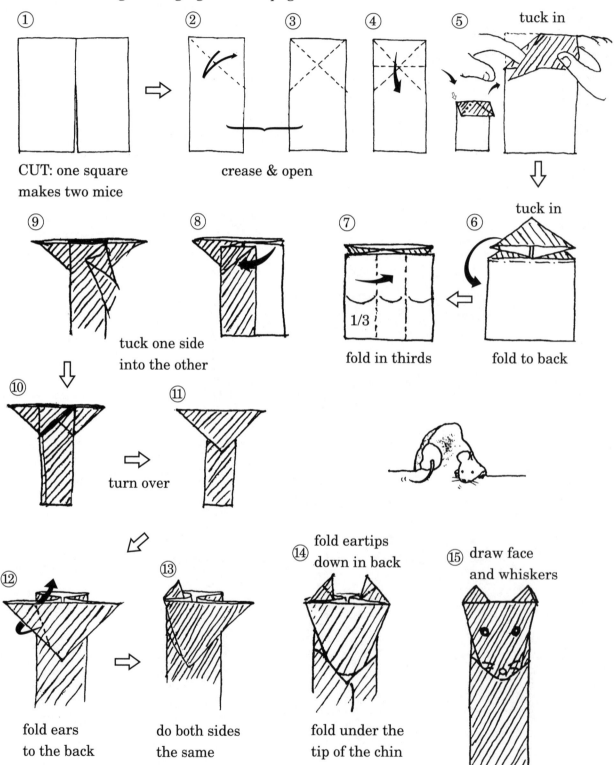

①
CUT: one square
makes two mice

② ③ crease & open

④

⑤ tuck in

⑥ tuck in
fold to back

⑦ 1/3
fold in thirds

⑧ tuck one side
into the other

⑨

⑩ turn over

⑪

⑫ fold ears
to the back

⑬ do both sides
the same

⑭ fold eartips
down in back
fold under the
tip of the chin

⑮ draw face
and whiskers

I Wish Today Was My Birthday!

You tell this story while showing the children the folded paper with birthday cake and animals.

Start by showing the side with Raccoon in the middle, under the birthday cake.

Raccoon said, "Today is my birthday! I am five years old today!"

Pig and Fox said, "Congratulations, Raccoon! Happy Birthday!"

But Fox thought, "I wish today was *my* birthday. I wish, I wish, I wish."

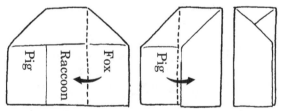

Close the paper, folding the Fox side in first, then the Pig side. Enclose the paper between your hands and wave them up and down while wishing.

But when you open your hands, take out the paper so that the other side faces the children.

Let's see whose birthday it is now. *Open. Fox should be in the middle now.*

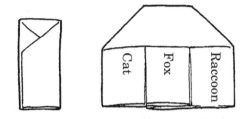

Oh! It is Fox's birthday! How old are you today, Fox?

Fox said, " I am five years old!"

Cat and Raccoon said, "Congratulations, Fox! Happy Birthday!"

But Cat thought, "I wish today was *my* birthday. I wish, I wish, I wish."

Close the paper, folding the Cat side in first, then the Raccoon side. Again enclose it in your hands while "wishing," and take it out showing the other side.

Let's see whose birthday it is now.

Ah! Now it is Cat's birthday! How old are you, Cat?

Cat said, "I am five years old today!"

Pig and Fox said, "Congratulations, Cat! Happy Birthday!"

But Pig thought, "I wish today was *my* birthday. I wish, I wish, I wish."

And so forth. You control whose birthday it is next by folding that one's side in first, then turning the paper over.

Of course you can adapt the number of candles to the age of your listeners.

Comment

Young children are delighted and mystified by the way the "birthday animal" changes every time you open the paper. The mystery depends on how well you hide the fact that you are turning the paper over. How long will it take the class wiz to figure it out?

For working with large groups, you can make a big, sturdy version out of cloth with painted or appliquéed animals.

Children can make their own "magic changers," drawing in any four items they wish. Examples: four flowers wanting sunshine; four toys wanting a child to play with them; four adult moods a child could wish for!

How To:

Materials: Plain paper, crayons or markers.

1. Fold the paper in half lengthwise. Open it; fold each long edge to the middle crease.

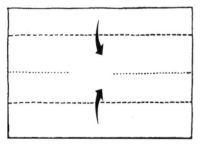

2. Refold along the original center crease.

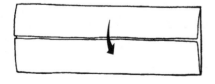

3. Fold down the right corner. You are measuring off the width along one long side.

4. Fold the remainder in half, up to the measuring part.

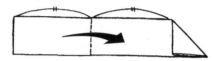

5. Unfold the right corner. Crease the left side up; unfold it.

6. Open the left side with your finger. Press it down flat, using the creases.

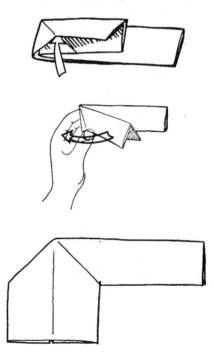

7. Fold the right side over the left, at the place shown.

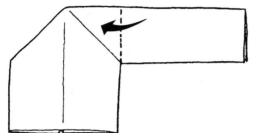

8. Crease down the upper (right) part, as in step 5. Unfold it, then open it and press it flat as in step 6.

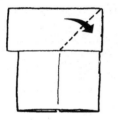

9. This is the back view of the house. Turn it over.

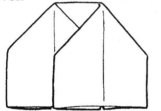

10. Front view. Draw the first three animals. Draw a birthday cake on the roof.

11. Draw Raccoon on the flap behind Cat. Turn the house over and draw an identical cake on the roof of the other side.

Doggie Policeman

Make milk carton hand puppets of the Doggie Policeman and the lost Kitty Cat. Move their mouths along with the words.

KC: Mew mew mew! *crying kitty*
DP: What's the matter with you?
KC: Mew mew mew!
DP: Do you have a pain somewhere in your body?
KC: Mew mew mew!
> *shaking head no,*
> *from side to side.*

DP: Did somebody tease you?
KC: Mew mew mew! *shaking head* No.
DP: Are you lost?
KC: Mew mew mew!
> *shaking head yes,*
> *up and down.*

DP: Oh, I see. What's your name?
KC: Mew mew mew!
> *shaking head no.*

DP: Well, can you tell me your address?
KC: Mew mew mew!
> *shaking head no.*

DP: What's your daddy's name?
KC: Mew mew mew!
> *shaking head no.*

DP: What's your mommy's name?
KC: Mew mew mew!
> *shaking head no.*

DP: What's your phone number?
KC: Mew mew mew!
> *shaking head no.*

DP: I've got a problem here ...
KC: Mew mew mew!
> *shaking head no.*

DP: I feel like crying, too!

How To:

Material: 2 milk cartons (pint or quart)
Tools: felt pen or crayons, scissors

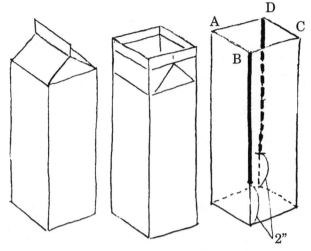

1. Open the top of the milk carton as shown.
2. Cut edges B and D down to 2" from the bottom.

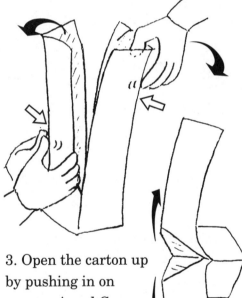

3. Open the carton up by pushing in on corners A and C, then folding the flaps back.
Open it very wide.

4. Draw the faces and bodies as shown, then cut off the excess carton.

Comment

This is an instant puppet show based on a popular song which most Japanese children already know. American children understand its humor even without the song.

Although other types of hand puppets would work, I like the milkcarton puppets best because you can open their mouths so wide when they cry!

After you demonstrate it once to the children, they will imitate it and want to start playing the puppet show immediately. Try making milk carton puppets for other familiar stories and songs.

What Kind of Egg Is This?

Tell this story while unfolding the paper hexagon over and over.

Start by showing the side with a drawing of an egg.

What kind of egg is this?

It must be kept warm for 21 days under the belly of the mother hen.

> *Fold the hexagon, open it from the middle to show the chick.*

And ... Yes, it's hatching into a chick.

That chick will eat leaves and grain, and grow big.

> *In the same way, open hexagon again to show the hen.*

Soon...Yes, it is becoming a hen.

She will eat worms and bugs and grain, and when she's big enough...

> *Open the hexagon again, showing the the egg.*

POINK! *(Sound of laying an egg)*

Yes, she will lay an egg.

What kind of egg is this?

> *You can repeat the cycle*

How To:

Material: a paper strip 6.5 times longer than it is wide (vis, 1.5" x 10")

Tools: scissors, glue, colored pencils.

"valley fold" (crease inside) ----------

"mountain fold" (crease up) – • – • – • –

turn the work over

1. Lightly crease one end of the strip in half lengthways to find the midline.

2. Fold the top corner down to this midline. Now the bottom corner is 60 degrees.

3. Turn the strip of paper over.

4. Fold the top corner down to the bottom.

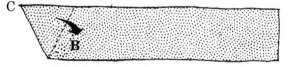

5. Turn the strip of paper over.

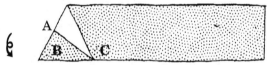

6. Fold the top corner down to the bottom.

7. Repeat until all the strip is folded.

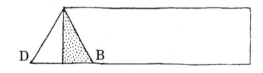

Now unfold the whole strip, and cut off extra.

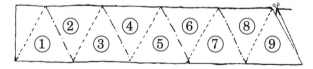

8. Refold as shown: at 3-4 and 6-7.

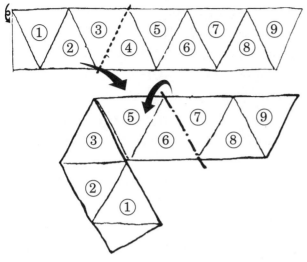

9. Glue the half-triangle from the beginning of the strip to the last (#9) triangle.

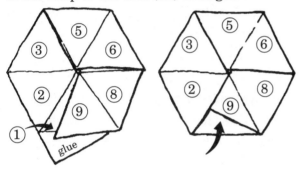

Draw an egg on the first surface.

To open the hexagon, keep A B C corners up and push the other corners down.

Now open the top from the middle.

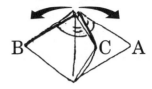

Draw a chick on this surface; open it again to draw the hen.

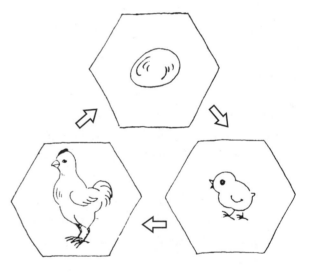

Comment

You could also make:
    Egg -> Caterpillar -> Butterfly
    Egg -> Tadpole -> Frog
    and so on.
Hmm, how would you do this with humans?

My Mommy Is Gone

Stand up the animal dolls made from tissue boxes, and tell the story.

The little boy fox was crying. His mommy wasn't there when he woke up.

A raccoon came to play with him.

Fox: Waah, waah, my mommy is gone!
Raccoon: Surely she just went shopping. Let's play a game drumming on my pot belly, and your mommy will come back. So stop crying.
PON POKO PON! *(Sound of drumming on belly)*
Fox: Waah, waah!
Raccoon: He won't stop crying, even when I drum on my belly. What shall I do?

A bear came.

Bear: What is the matter with you?
Raccoon: He said his mommy is gone, and I drummed on my belly, but he won't stop crying.
Bear: She should get back soon. Don't cry. Here, I'll give you a little of my honey. You can wait for her while we eat this honey together.
Fox: Waah, waah!
Bear: Don't you like honey? What shall I do?

A little rabbit passed by.

Rabbit: What's the matter with you?
Raccoon: He said his mommy is gone, and I drummed on my belly but he won't stop crying.

Rabbit: Well, I will show you my Boing Boing dance, so stop crying.
BOING BOING BOING BOING
BOING BOING BOING BOING
BOING BOING BOING BOING
Fox: Waah, waah!
Rabbit: He never stops crying, even when I do my Boing Boing dance. What shall I do?

Then a little monkey came.

Monkey: What's the matter with you?
Raccoon: He says his mommy is gone. I drummed on my belly, Bear gave him some honey, and Rabbit showed him the Boing Boing dance, but he won't stop crying.
Monkey: OK, I will climb up the tree and look for your mommy for you.
SURU SURU SURU
move monkey doll up high,
above listeners' heads or on a shelf
Oh, Fox's mommy is on her way back to the house with a lot of strawberries.
Fox: Really?
Monkey: Yes, it's true, here she is!
Fox's Mother: Hello! I picked a lot of strawberries. Let's eat them together.

Then, the mothers of Raccoon, Bear, Rabbit, and Monkey also came to see why their children had not come home on time. They all ate strawberries together!

Comment

You can put these tissue box or paper sack animal dolls on your hands and use them for puppets, or just stand them on a table. Of course you can use stuffed toy animals, too.

Story and characters are flexible, so you can play this easily with whatever animal dolls or toys you have handy.

How To:

Material: 5 facial tissue boxes or paper lunch sacks
Animal face pictures on stiff paper.
Tools: paints, crayons, scissors, glue

1. Open end flaps of tissue box.
2. Fold flaps to the inside.

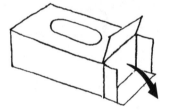

If you want to make the box shorter, cut off the end-flaps, cut along the corners, fold in.

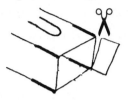

3. Make a dent in each side.
4. Fold the closed end down.

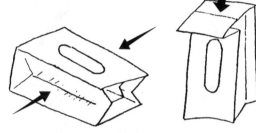

5. Glue on the animal faces.

Turkey Lake

You tell this story while adding more lines to the picture until it becomes a — surprise!

1. Long ago, there was a beautiful lake on the prairie.

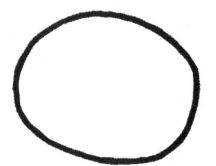

2. Fish swam in the lake.

3. Ducks and geese came to the lake.

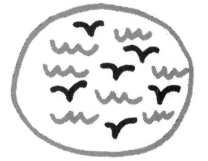

4. Sometimes the Indian people set up their teepees and camped by this lake.

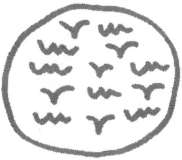

5. They walked to the lake to get fresh water.

6. They walked to the lake to catch fish. It was a beautiful place to camp.

7. One day, a family of pioneers built their round dugout house near the lake.

9. One day, they looked out the little round window in the wall of their house.

8. They too walked to the lake to get fresh water and to catch fish.

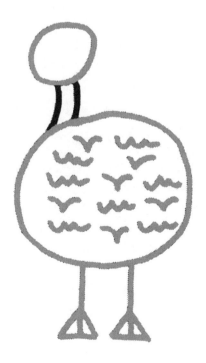

10. "Oh, no!" they shouted. "The ducks and geese are flying south for the winter! Now what can we have for our Thanksgiving dinner?"

11. They opened the door to run outside.
And that's when they saw...

12. Something tastier than a duck or goose!
They saw a big plump TURKEY! They had a
wonderful Thanksgiving dinner. So now every
year they have turkey for Thanksgiving.

Comment

I learned this story from Oklahoma storyteller Fran Stallings, who developed it from an idea her children found in one of Laura Ingalls Wilder's "Little House" books.

And Then, And Then

Rain Hat

You tell this story while folding newspapers into many different shapes. You will need three sheets of newspaper, tape, and a pair of scissors.

1. It was a rainy day. Momma said I couldn't go outside to play because the rain would get me wet. So I made a rain hat out of a sheet of newspaper, like this:

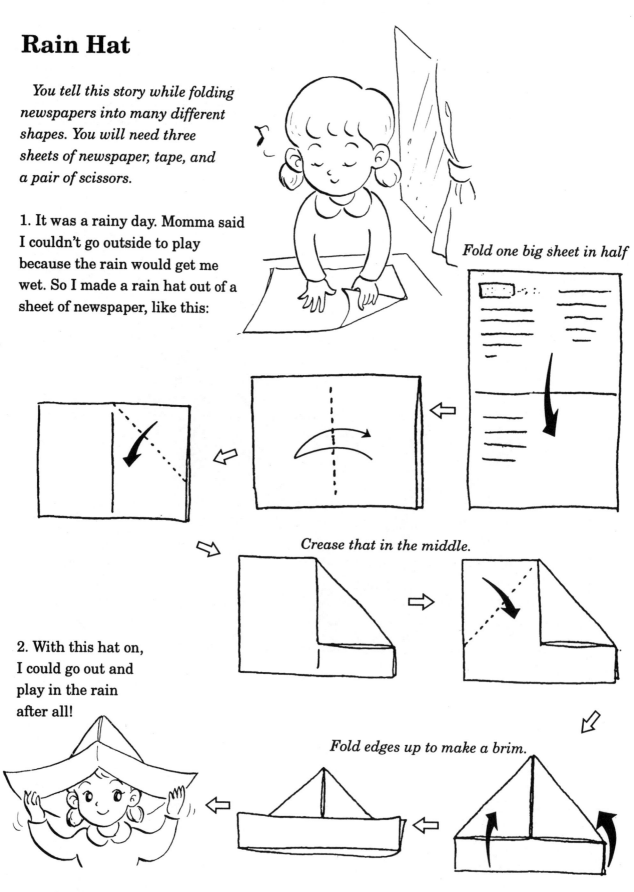

Fold one big sheet in half

Crease that in the middle.

Fold edges up to make a brim.

2. With this hat on, I could go out and play in the rain after all!

3. I splashed in puddles and watched the rain running down the street. But then I saw that a building was on fire! How exciting! I wanted to help, but I needed a fire-fighters' hat.

Open the hat

The starred corner will come to the front

Tuck the brim corners one under the other.

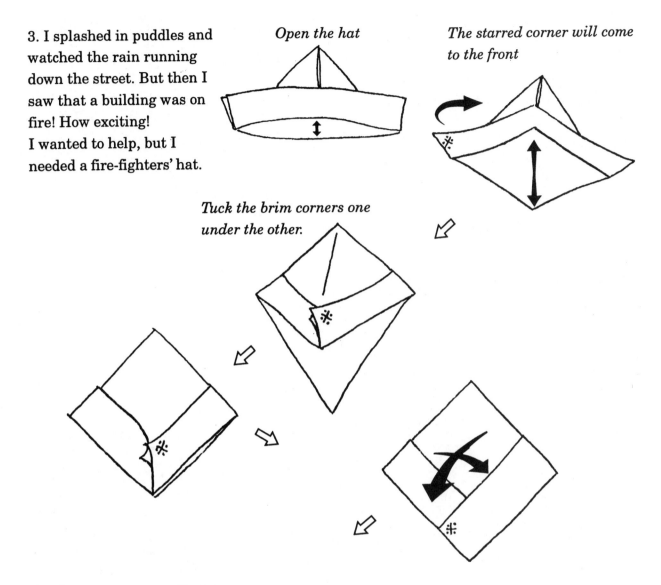

Fold one corner up to the top.

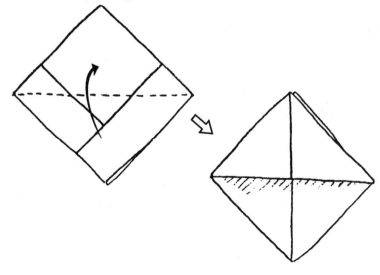

4. I made my rain hat into a fire-fighter's hat. Now I could fight the fire!

5. I needed a hose to pour water on the fire.

You need two more sheets of newspaper. Roll them up together, overlapping by several inches.

Fasten the roll firmly with tape 2" from each end.

6. Whoosh! Swoosh! I poured water on the fire from my fire hose.

7. Oh no! Someone was trapped on the top floor of the burning building! They were calling for help! How could I save them? I needed a hook and ladder truck!

Help!

8. I used my fire hose to make a ladder.

Cut out and remove the shaded part (more than half the width). Leave 4" at each end for handles. One person holds the handles, ends turned down. Another person pulls up the "rungs" of the ladder — very slowly and gently.

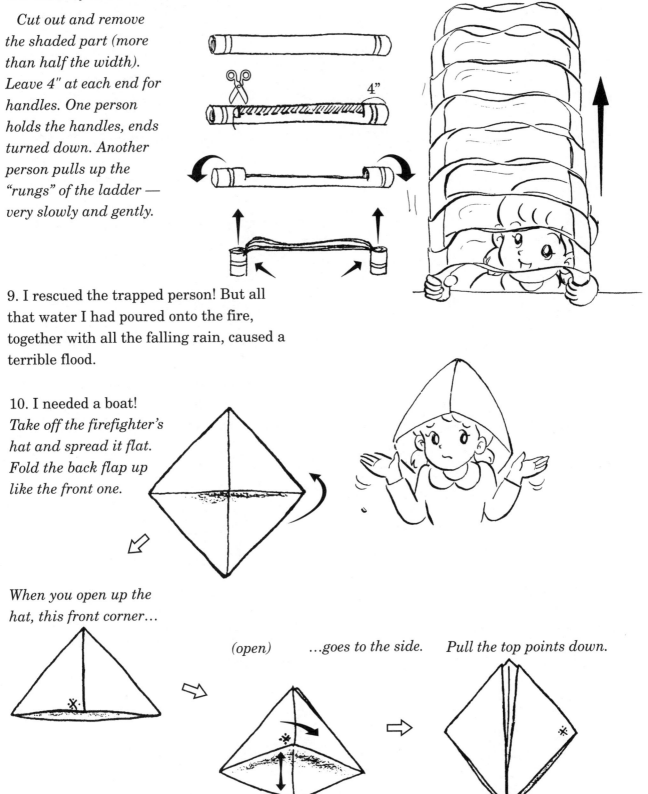

9. I rescued the trapped person! But all that water I had poured onto the fire, together with all the falling rain, caused a terrible flood.

10. I needed a boat! *Take off the firefighter's hat and spread it flat. Fold the back flap up like the front one.*

When you open up the hat, this front corner…

(open)   *…goes to the side.*   *Pull the top points down.*

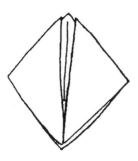
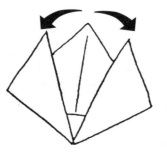

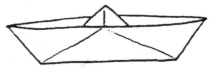

11. So I had a boat to escape the flood. I sailed all over town.

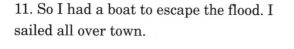

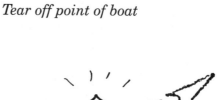

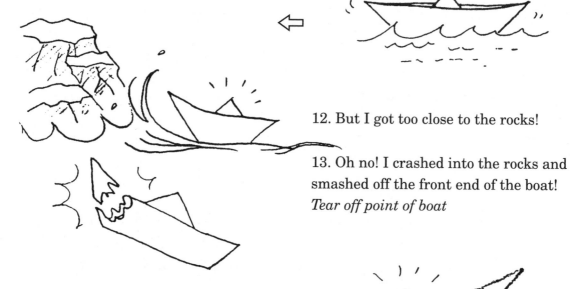

12. But I got too close to the rocks!

13. Oh no! I crashed into the rocks and smashed off the front end of the boat!
Tear off point of boat

14. Then a huge wave came along ...

... and smashed off the other end of the boat!
Tear off other point of boat

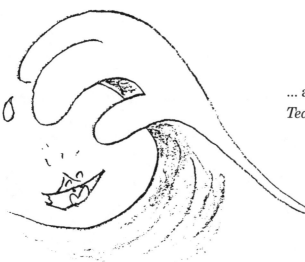

15. Thunder crashed and lightning struck our boat, smashing off the middle point.

Here's how the boat looks with its missing pieces.

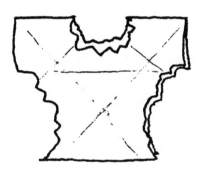

16. Oh no, the boat was sinking! I was going to drown!
But don't worry …
Turn away from the audience, unfold the boat, and …

It's a life jacket. Put it on.

17. **I had a life jacket!**

Comment

I learned this story in America from Fran Stallings, than added the hose and the ladder part myself. I think extending the fire ladder is fun.

Fran Stallings adds: And I learned it from California storyteller Nancy Schimmel, who says a little girl taught it to her at the public library one rainy day.

The Old Coat

Prepare the drawings shown on page 49. Show them to the children as you tell the story. (You can also tell the story without pictures.)

Show the front side of the paper, the coat.

A long time ago, a man made himself a coat. But after he wore it for many years, it got so worn-out he couldn't wear it any more.
Fold the paper in half to show the jacket drawn on one side of the back.

So he remade the coat into a jacket. But after he wore it for many years, it got so worn-out he couldn't wear it any more.
Fold in half to show the vest.

So he remade the jacket into a vest. But after he wore it for many years, it got so worn-out he couldn't wear it any more.
Fold in half to show the cap.

So he remade the vest into a cap. But after he wore it for many years, it got so worn-out he couldn't wear it any more.
Fold in half to show the tie.

So he remade the cap into a tie. But after he wore it for many years, it got so worn-out he couldn't wear it any more.
Fold in half to show the button.

So he rolled the tie up into a button. But after he wore it for many years, it got so worn-out he couldn't use it any more.
Fold in half to show a blank.

And then what do you think he made next? He made this story. And stories *never* wear out.

Comment

I heard this story from American storyteller Fran Stallings. When she asked the last time, "What do you think he made from the button?" I tried to imagine something even smaller than a button.

When she said, "He made a story, and the story never wore out," I groaned because I had not guessed that.

But this is true. A story doesn't get worn out, and can be passed from someone to Fran, and from Fran to me, and from me to you. I feel that even in such a short story, there is "the soul of the story," so I love this story very much.

Fran Stallings adds: This story is very popular with American storytellers, and I often use it when training beginners and children. I think the original English source may be Nancy Schimmel's adaptation of a Yiddish folksong, which became the title story in her handbook *Just Enough to Make a Story* (Sisters' Choice Books, 1982)

How to:

Materials: a sheet of paper as big as possible (<u>use both sides</u>).
Tools: paint or crayons

Fold the paper to measure off halves as shown, and draw the pictures.

One Is Missing!

You can tell this story with ten origami piglets.

There were ten piglet brothers. One day they wanted to take a walk all by themselves, without any grownup pigs.

Their mother said, "One of you might get lost if you walk separately. Stay together, and make sure nobody gets lost."

So before they left home, they decided to count each other to make sure all ten were there.

The first piglet tried to count.

"One, two, three, four, five, six, seven, eight, nine—one piglet is missing! Oink oink oink!"

The second piglet tried to count.

"One, two, three, four, five, six, seven, eight, nine—Oink oink oink! Who on earth is missing?"

The third pig tried.

"One, two, three, four, five, six, seven, eight, nine—one piglet is missing! Oink oink oink! Red piglet is here, blue piglet is here, yellow piglet is here— "

Each one tried to count, but there was always one piglet missing! At last, before they could take their walk, it grew dark.

If children are not satisfied with this ending, you can add:

Their mother pig came along and said, "What's the matter?"

"Someone is missing!"

"Oh really! I will count you myself. One, two, three, four, five, six, seven, eight, nine, ten. You are all here, all ten!"

And then the piglets went on their walk.

Comment

This story is enjoyed very much by children who have just learned to count. Older children will enjoy learning to count in other languages. They can also learn the color words, the word for "pig" (or other animal), for Mother, et cetera.

Make ten origami paper piglets, arrange them in a row, and tell the story.

Variations: use only five piglets. Or use other animals, such as kittens or puppies.

How to:

For each piglet, you need one piece of origami paper or other light paper, <u>perfectly</u> <u>square.</u>

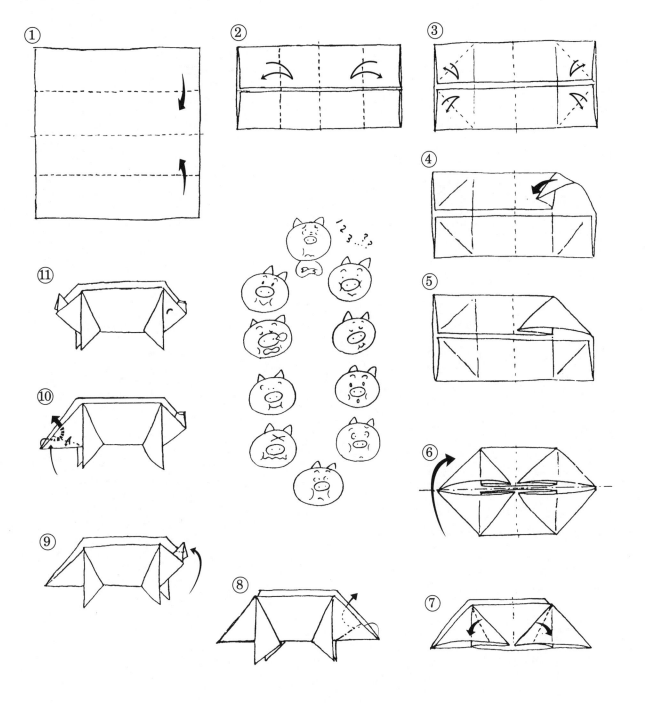

Mountain Climbing

Tell this story while folding newspaper.
Have two sheets of newspaper ready.

2. How hot it is! I will put on my hat.
Fold that sheet of newspaper into the shape
of a hat. Bend the brim to front and back.
Put it on your head.

1. Let's climb that mountain!
Fold one sheet of newspaper diagonally.

3. I need a walking stick.
*Make a tube with the other
sheet of newspaper.*

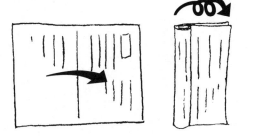

4. I am thirsty. I will drink water
from the mountain stream.
*Unroll the "walking stick" and fold
it into a cup. First, fold one corner
down diagonally to measure off a
square. Fold the extra paper to the
inside.*

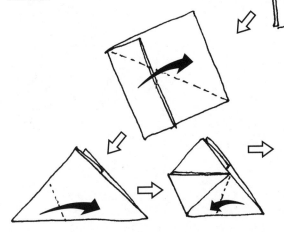

How tasty the mountain water is!

5. Oh! A bird is singing! What kind of bird is it?
I will look through my binoculars.
Unfold cup, roll both sides to the middle.

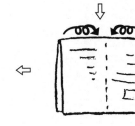

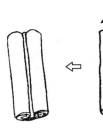

6. Now I'll climb some more.
Make the walking stick again.

7. How hot it is! I will take a rest.
Unroll the walking stick, and pleat the paper into a fan. Fold the fan in half.

What a nice wind!

8. I love the mountain scenery. Oh, butterflies are flying!
Pinch the pleated fan by the middle, shake it gently to "fly".

9. The scenery is so pretty here, I will pitch my tent and camp.
Take off the hat, and make it into a tent.

10. I will go get water from the mountain stream.

Ouch! I slipped and sprained my ankle! I can't walk! I'm in trouble!

11. No problem, I'll go home by airplane! *Make an airplane by folding the tent in half, then fold the wings.*

Comment

Newspaper is a handy material which is readily available and free. You can make a paper snap-popper, or roll a sheet into a tube "rope" to play tug-of-war; wad it into a ball to play catch, or use an unfolded sheet as a bridge for others to pass under. These are all fun activities to play with newspaper.

Now, can you use these and other newspaper shapes to make up new stories?

Burglar's Hideout

Prepare an envelope as the burglar's hideout with a window. Tell the story using cards for the burglar and the lady.

How to:

Materials: 2 index cards
1 envelope a little larger than cards.
Tools: knife, scissors, colored pencils or markers, glue.

1. Draw the picture of the burglar on one card and cut out the shaded area.
2. Stack the second card under the first one and trace the shape of the cutout onto it in pencil.
3. Draw the picture of the lady on the bottom card. Draw her eyes and half nose in the outlined area, then erase the pencil outline.
4. Stack the picture of the burglar on top of the picture of the lady; check the color balance and fit.
5. Stack the burglar card on top of the envelope and trace the cutout area with pencil.
6. Cut both layers of the envelope <u>a little smaller</u> than the traced area, to make windows in the hideout.

Long ago there was a burglar so tricky that he had never been caught. He could steal quickly and he could run away fast. Even the police couldn't catch him. This is his hideout.

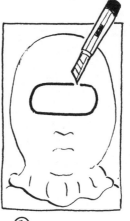

①

④

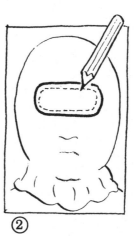

②

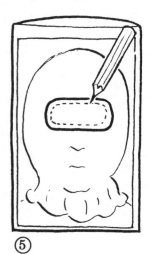

③

⑤

⑥

Show the envelope with the "burglar" (both cards) inside. We can see only his eyes and nose.

"Well, I guess I'll go to work tonight." At night, the burglar went out to steal things. *Take the burglar (both cards held firmly together) out of the envelope hideout, and move him around a little.*

But a policeman with a night-stick spotted him and ran after him. *You can make a paper cutout policeman, or use the index finger of your other hand.*

"Oh, no!" The burglar ran off in a hurry and hid in his hideout. *Quickly put the burglar back into the envelope.*

The policeman ran after him frantically, and saw him enter his hideout. The policeman said to himself, "OK, I will wait here and keep watch. When he comes out of that house, I will catch him." And the policeman watched from behind a tree.

The burglar looked out of the window and said, "That policemen is watching me. I'd better be careful." *Have your policeman watch the envelope hideout intently. Turn the envelope slightly so that it seems to watch the policeman.*

"He is still watching me. I have no choice but to use a disguise." And so the burglar dressed up as a beautiful lady and came out of the hideout. *Take out just the back card, of the lady. Move her over to the policeman.*

The beautiful lady said, "Hello, officer. Thank you for doing such a good job of

keeping the streets safe." The policeman was embarrased at the lady's attention.
Set the lady card down.

"How strange!" thought the policeman. "Certainly that burglar went into this house. I will peek inside."
Put your eye to the window of the envelope and peek inside.
Even put your finger through the hole to show listeners that the hideout is empty.

"Oh, it's empty! I thought the burglar went in here, but I must have made a mistake."

The policeman went away, still looking puzzled. He figured he had made a mistake.

The burglar said, "Now the policeman has gone away and I have time until dawn. So I can go to work."

Put the lady card back into the envelope — behind the burglar card. Now take out both cards and move the burglar away on his rounds.

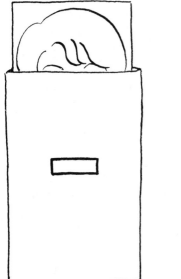

Comment

You must hold both cards together firmly or the trick will be discovered by your watchful audience. Also, make sure you don't have strong light behind you: light may shine through the single layer in the area of the eyes.

Variation

This is Santa Claus' house. "Mr. Santa, Mr. Santa, Christmas Day is coming soon. Will you grant my wish? I want ——"
Bring out Mrs. Santa (back card only).

"Mr. Santa is not here. You know there are still ____ days until Christmas. If you are good until then, Mr. Santa will surely grant your request. Why don't you wait at home?"
"What? Are you sure? Is Mr. Santa really not here?"
Use finger to show that the house is "empty."

"Oh, he really is not at home. How strange. We have no choice, we must go home and wait."
"Well well, the children went home, I can take a nap."
Return Mrs. Santa to the house.

And then on Christmas eve, Mr. Santa comes out.
"Ho! Ho! Ho!"
Bring out both cards, held firmly together.

Dandelion

Make the paper dandelion and let many kinds of animals visit it. You can use stuffed animals, picture cards, et cetera.

On the side of the road there was a dandelion.

Its yellow flower shone and glowed in the sunlight.

A child came.

"**Dan** delion!"

The child poked at it with her finger.

The dandelion nodded its head and said, "Hello."

A dog came.

"**Woof** delion!"

The dog put his nose close to the dandelion and smelled it.

The dandelion nodded its head and said, "Hello."

A cat came.

"**Meow** delion!"

The cat rubbed her whiskers on the dandelion.

The dandelion nodded its head and said, "Hello."

A sparrow came.

"**Chirp** delion!"

The sparrow picked at its leaf.

The dandelion nodded its head and said, "Hello."

A snake came.

"..............."

The snake curled silently around the dandelion.

The dandelion nodded its head and said, "Hello."

Today the dandelion was able to say hello to many people.

So the dandelion was happy.

How to:

Materials: yellow and green paper.
Tools: tape, scissors.

<u>Flowers</u>: Cut yellow paper in thirds. Fold each strip in half, fringe from the folded edge. Roll up and secure with tape.

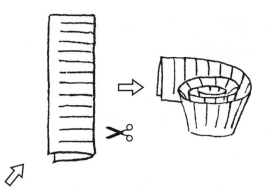

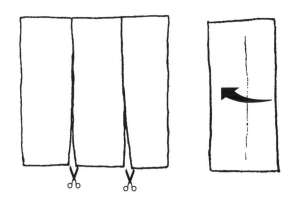

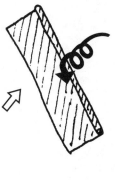

<u>Foliage</u>: Cut green paper in half. Shape leaves from one half. Roll the other half into a thin tube to make the stalk.

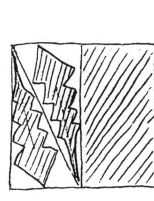

Open the blossom and fluff out its petals.

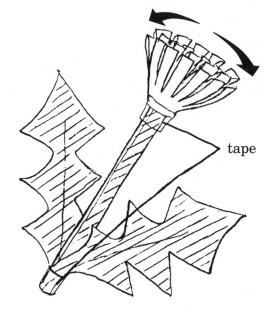

tape

Comment

I invented this story with Japanese children. While we were taking a walk, the children found dandelions and said,"Oh, *Tanpopo! Tanpopo!*" (dandelion)

But child A, who was catching a cold, said *"Danpopo!"*

Everyone laughed. A. was embarassed.

So B. said to A., "An elephant named Danbo calls *Tanpopo* **'Danpopo'**."

"Well, what do dogs call *Tanpopo?*"

*"**Wan**popo!"* (wan = woof)

"Well, how about cats?"

*"**Nyan**popo!" (*nyan = meow)

That's how this story developed.

Any animals can appear in this story. You can used stuffed animals or animal pictures. If you save a voiceless animal for the end, it adds a funny twist.

The Only Thing I Am Afraid Of Is —

You tell this story while holding up and turning over the cards one after another.

Show the card of a mouse, side A.
I am a mouse. I am the strongest of mice. The only thing I am afraid of is —
Bring out the card with the cat, side A.

CATS!
"Meow!"
The mouse runs away.
Turn over the mouse card to side B; run it away, put it down.

I am a cat. I am the strongest of cats. The only thing I am afraid of is —
Bring out the card with the dog, side A.

DOGS!
"Bow wow!"
The cat runs away.
Turn over the cat card to side B; run it away, put it down.

I am a dog. I am the strongest of dogs. The only thing I am afraid of is —
Bring out the woman's card, side A.

MY OWNER!
"Bad dog! What are you doing!!"
The dog runs away.
Turn over the dog card to side B; run it away, put it down.

I am a woman. I am the strongest one in my family. The only thing I am afraid of is—
Bring out the card with the mouse again, side A.

MICE!
"Squeak!"
The woman runs away.
Turn over the woman's card to side B; run it away, put it down.

I am a mouse. I am the strongest of mice. The only thing I am afraid of is —

CATS!
"Meow!"
… and so on, as you like. The story is endless.

How to:

Materials: 8 pieces of stiff paper
4 sticks (popsicle or craft sticks)
Tools: paints or crayons, stapler, tape,
scissors, glue, paper clips.

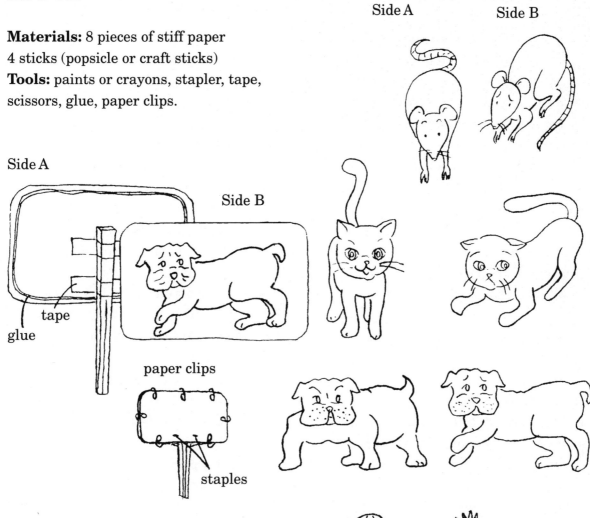

Side A

Side B

tape

glue

paper clips

staples

1. Draw 8 pictures as shown on the right.
2. Glue one stick on the back of A, and tape
it on for good measure.
3. Glue A and B together, back to back,
with the stick inside.
4. Staple A & B together near the stick to
secure it.
5. Paperclip A & B together until the glue
has dried.

Cluck Cluck Hen

This story goes with a hen, two eggs, and two chicks made from cotton gloves.
Hide the eggs inside the hen. Put the chicks in the basket, cover them with the hen. Then put the basket into a cloth bag.

There is someone in this bag. But I think she is still asleep.
Peek into the bag.

Let's wake her up: *sing*
Cluck, cluck, it's daytime.
Cluck, cluck, wake up!

Oh, she woke up! Let's see who it is.
Show a bit of the hen's head.

That's right. This is a hen.
Take the hen out of the bag (leave the basket inside). Set her on the palm of one hand and pet her back with the other.

Now let's sing a song so that the hen will lay eggs for us.
Hen, hen
Can you lay us some eggs?
Reach under the hen and pull out one egg.

Poink! Look, she laid an egg!
Usually she lays just one egg a day, but if everyone sings together, today she may lay another one for us.
Hen, hen
Can you lay us some eggs?
Reach under and pull out the other egg.

Poink! Look, she laid another egg!
Put the hen back inside the bag setting her onto the basket, hiding the chicks. Now bring out basket and hen together. Show the children how you tuck the eggs under the belly of the setting hen.
Put the basket in your lap.

The hen will sit on these eggs and keep them warm for twenty-one days. Because we can't wait that long, let's just clap *softly* 21 times.
Lead children in clapping and counting.

One, two, — twenty, twenty-one.

Peep peep peep peep!
Look, the egg hatched into a cute chick!
Take a chick out from under the hen and put it on her back, tucked in a wing.

What about the other egg?
Peep peep peep peep!
Oh, it became a cute chick too!
Take out the other chick and tuck it into the hen's wing.

Congratulations, Mama Hen!

How to:

Materials:
cotton gloves, 1 white 1 yellow
black beads, stuffing
felt scraps white, orange, red.
Tools: needle, thread, glue

white glove:

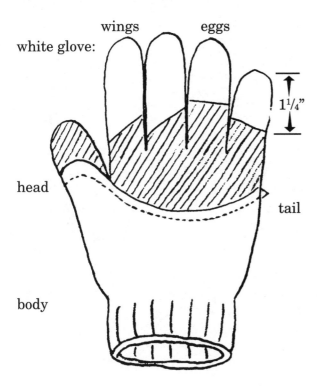

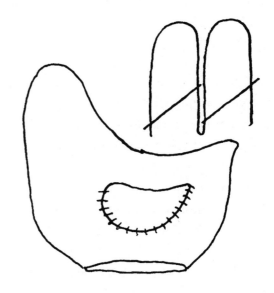

discard

cutting line ————————

sewing line - - - - - - - -

4. Cut off wings (index and middle finger, cut as shown) and sew them to the body as shown, sewing on <u>bottom</u> edge only — this makes a pocket to hold the chicks.

1. **Hen**: Turn the glove inside-out. Sew the line from head to tail, cut off excess (leave a 1/4 inch seam allowance).

2. Turn it rightside out and stuff the head and body. Leave some space in the belly so you can hide eggs.

3. You can cut and pull out the elastic threads in the wrist.

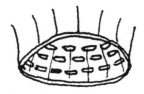

5. Decorate the hen by sewing on a yellow felt beak (two triangles), red felt crest, and bead eyes.

6. **Eggs**: Cut off the pinky and ring finger-tips of the white glove, each 1 1/4" long. Stuff each one. Gather the open ends lightly, then tuck in the cut edges and gather tightly into a ball.

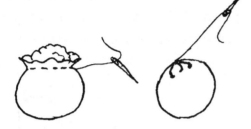

7. **Chicks** are made from the fingertips of the yellow glove. Procede as for eggs. For a cuter shape, lightly draw up a line of gathering stitches to make a dent.

Add orange bills and black thread eyes. Feet (optional) = orange triangles.

7. Prepare a basket not too much bigger than the hen.

8. Prepare a drawstring bag for the hen to "sleep" in (and for storage of all parts).

Hanky Stories

Tell these stories while making many different shapes out of handkerchiefs. Have two handkerchiefs ready.

1. Here is the Hanky Family's house. Roses are blooming in the garden.

2. Papa Hanky wears a tie when he goes to work.

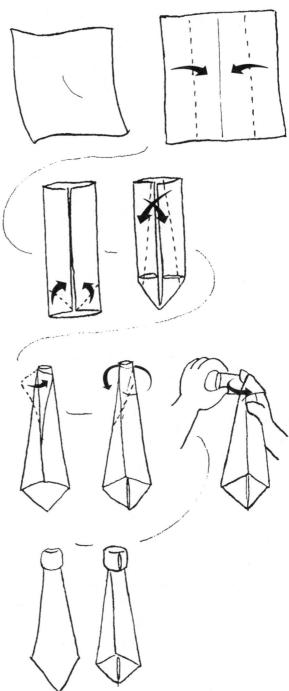

3. Mama Hanky wears an apron when she cooks.

4. Grandma Hanky is sewing something with her needle.

Move your hand as if holding a needle.

5. Brother Hanky's afternoon snack is a tasty banana.

Pinch corners and bottom layer.

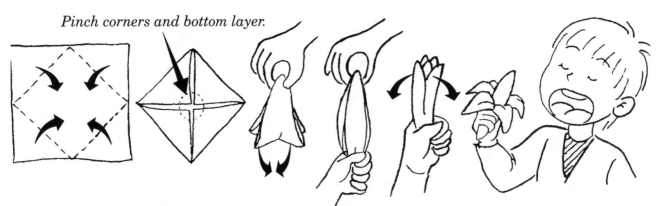

6. Sister Hanky plays with her doll.

Pinch in to make the neck.

7. Her doll is lonely, so she makes another doll.

Comment

You can tell this story to five or six children at a time, while you fold the handkerchiefs on a table or the carpet. If you can provide extra handkerchiefs for the children to experiment with, they can join in the play.

A Pile of Stuff

This story goes with cards that have pictures on both sides.

Show the front of the first card.

One day, a group of children were taking a walk. In the middle of the road there was a big pile of stuff.

"Mister, Mister, why don't you carry this away?"

"I can't take this away because my horse is too skinny and weak."

Show the front of the second card.

"Horse, Horse, why are you skinny and weak?"

"I can't put on weight because the grass isn't growing."

Show the front of the third picture.

"Grass, Grass, why don't you grow?"

"I can't grow because the rain doesn't fall."

Show the front of the fourth card.

"Rain, Rain, why don't you fall?"

"I can't fall because a cloud doesn't come."

Show the front of the fifth card.

"Cloud, Cloud, why don't you come?"

"I can't come because the wind isn't blowing."

Show the front of the sixth card.

"Wind, Wind, why don't you blow?"

"I can't blow because—nobody is singing!"

Turn the sixth picture over.

And then the children sang a song.

The wind heard the song and began to blow happily.

Turn the fifth picture over.

The cloud was blown by the wind and flew smoothly.

Turn the fourth picture over.

The rain began to fall heavily from the cloud.

Turn the third picture over.

The grass received the rain and grew steadily.

Turn the second picture over.

The horse ate the grass, put on weight and grew strong.

How to:

Materials: paper for drawing, stiff paper for cards.
Tools: crayons, markers, glue.

Turn the first picture over.

The man loaded his stuff on the horse and they carried it away.

And the children continued on their walk.

Comment

Children will enjoy this story if you just tell it. But if you are good at singing, when you get to "And then the children sang a song," you can sing something that would make the wind want to blow. This will make the story more interesting—especially if your listeners can sing along.

Bend the stiff paper to make standing cards as shown. Put pictures on both sides.

Front

Back

The Stories Go
On And On

Wide-Mouth Frog

You tell this story with a frog handpuppet made from a milk carton.

A long time ago there was a young wide-mouth frog who wanted to know everything.

One day the frog asked her mother, "Mom, what do other animals eat?"

The mother said, "Well, I don't know, honey. Why don't you go ask them? But when you ask someone something, you should be polite. Don't forget to introduce yourself. You are a frog with a big mouth. So throw out your chest and say, 'I am a little wide-mouth frog.' Okay?"

"I understand, Mom," said the little wide-mouth frog. And she hopped into the woods.

She met a bear.

"Excuse me, Mr. Bear, may I ask you something?

What is your favorite food?"

"My favorite foods are nuts or fish. Best of all I like honey."

"Thank you, Mr. Bear. Oh, I forgot to introduce myself. I am a wide-mouth frog."

The frog threw out her chest as she said this, and then hopped into the deep woods.

She met a little bird.

"Excuse me, Ms. Bird, may I ask you something?

What is your favorite food?"

"I like worms or seeds. I like worms or seeds. I like worms or seeds. I like —" she chirped, and flew away.

"Thank you, Ms. Bird. Oh, I forgot to introduce myself. I am a wide-mouth frog."

The frog threw out her chest as she said this, and then hopped further into the deep woods.

She met a deer.

"Excuse me, Ms. Deer, may I ask you something? What is your favorite food?"

"I like grass or leaves. In winter I eat tree bark," the deer answered

"Thank you, Ms. Deer. Oh, I almost forgot to introduce myself. I am a wide-mouth frog."

The frog threw out her chest as she said

this, and then hopped through the deep woods into the swamp.

In the swamp, she met an alligator.

"Excuse me, Mr. Alligator, may I ask you something? What is your favorite food?"

The alligator answered in a scary voice, "You want to know my favorite food, little lady? My favorite food is — wide-mouth frogs! I like them very much. Have you seen any around here?"

As he spoke, he crept closer to her.

"No, no, Mr. Alligator. I have never seen such frogs before. I am a *small*-mouth frog. A *small*-mouth frog. Good bye!"

The little wide-mouth frog went home in a hurry.

Sometimes it is good to keep your wide mouth *shut*.

How To:

Materials: 1 milk carton
Tools: felt tip pens, scissors.

Make the frog handpuppet like Doggie Policeman on page 32.

Move the mouth widely when the frog talks — except at the end, when the mouth hardly opens!

Mouse's Marriage

You tell this story with finger-puppet mice and pictures on cards.

Once upon a time there was a mother mouse, a father mouse, and their daughter Chuuko. Chuuko was old enough to marry, so her parents were looking for a husband. They wanted the greatest husband in the world for her.

Mother and Father Mouse thought the sun was the greatest, because the sun rises to the highest place and shines over all the world. So they went to the sun.

"Mr. Sun, Mr. Sun, greatest sun in the world, would you like to marry our daughter?"

"Oh, I am afraid you are mistaken. I shine on all the world, but when a cloud comes, it can stop my shining. I am no match for a cloud."

Then Mother and Father Mouse went to a cloud.

"Mr. Cloud, Mr. Cloud, greatest cloud in the world, would you like to marry our daughter?"

"Oh, I am afraid you are mistaken. I float grandly in the sky, but when the wind comes, it blows me away. I am no match for the wind."

Then Mother and Father Mouse went to the wind.

"Mr. Wind, Mr. Wind, greatest wind in the world, would you like to marry our daughter?"

"Oh, I am afraid you are mistaken. I blow hard, but when I run into a wall, I can go no further. I am no match for a wall."

So Mother and Father Mouse went to a wall.

Mr. Wall, Mr. Wall, greatest wall in the world, would you like to marry our daughter?"

"Oh, I am afraid you are mistaken. I am tough, but when a mouse bites me, it can easily make a hole. I am no match for a mouse."

They thought, the greatest husband in the world is a mouse.

So they went to the handsome young mouse Chuuta who lived next door.

"Mr. Chuuta, Mr. Chuuta, greatest mouse in the world, would you like to marry our daughter?"

Chuuta was very glad to be asked. He and Chuuko were married and lived happy ever after.

How To:

Materials: a sheet of stiff paper
Tools: paints or crayons, scissors.

Cut the paper into fourths and draw the sun, cloud, wind, and wall.

You can use the mouse finger puppets or origami mice from **Squeak Squeak Squeak** (page 26).

To enhance the wedding atmosphere, you can put a bit of white veil on Chuuko and a bowtie on Chuuta (Velcro® is handy).

I Want ...

Draw the pictures on a long, long strip of paper rolled into a scroll. Tell the story while unrolling it a little at a time. (See photo page 73.)

In English, we have pairs of words that sound similar but mean different things, like "meet" and "meat." We like to tell funny stories about mix-ups caused by these words (like Amelia Bedelia). Japanese has words like this, too. For instance, *"hoshi"* means "star," but *"hoshii"* means "I want."

Let the children practice saying these words. "Hoshi" (stars) is clipped off short but "hoshii..." (I want) is drawn out long.

Very good! Now here's a funny story about those two words.

A long time ago there was a very selfish little prince. Unless he got his way at once, he complained and complained. If the prince wanted fish, his father the king told the fisherman to catch some fish. If the prince wanted roast duck, the king told the hunters to shoot ducks. The prince could get anything he wanted.

One day the prince said, *"Are ga, hoshii...! (That over there, I want it...)."*

The king said, "Yes, my boy, of course you can have it!" and he told his servant to get it at once.

First the servant made a road up the highest mountain in their country...

(show pictures 1 and 2)
and then he built a five-storied pagoda...
(show pictures 3, 4, 5)
and then he fastened a ladder on the top of the pagoda...
(picture 6)
and then he fastened another ladder on the end of the first ladder...
(picture 7)
and then he fastened a third ladder on the end of that one...
(picture 8)
and then the tallest servant in the castle climbed the ladders...
(picture 9)
and then the king got onto the head of that servant...
(picture 10)
and the king held the prince in his arms.
(picture 11)
Then the prince tried to take what he wanted with a long leafy bamboo pole...
(pictures 12, 13)
But he still could not get that thing which he wanted...
(open picture 14...)
Well, guess what the prince wanted? What did he say *"hoshii... hoshii..."* about?

Let the children guess. If they answer "the sun" or "the moon", you can repeat, "the thing he said hoshii... hoshii... about," shortening the end so that it sounds more like "hoshi" (star).

When they answer "star" you confirm this by opening to picture 15.

How To:

Materials: 18 sheets of paper
Tools: markers or crayons, tape, glue.

1. Put 15 pieces of paper together vertically (short sides together).
2. Add a piece on either side of the first sheet.

3. Cut the remaining piece in half, and put the halves on either side of the second sheet.
4. Draw the 15 scenes as shown. You don't have to draw anything for the 14th scene.
5. Roll it up with the narrow top inside, and the wide bottom outside.

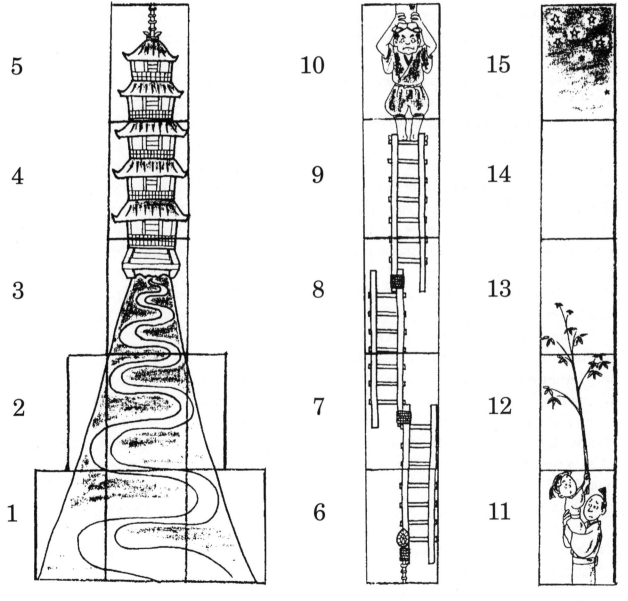

5
4
3
2
1

10
9
8
7
6

15
14
13
12
11

That's Totally True

You tell this story while encouraging listeners to chime in rhythmically, "Yes, that's to-tally true." Before you start, you may want to ask them to practice chanting this together with you.

Optional: *invite them to chant this line in the original Japanese: "Haa, sono tori!"*

Once upon a time, there was a rich man whose daughter was so beautiful that a great many young men sought her hand in marriage.

Because the rich man loved listening to stories, he said, "I will give my daughter to the man who can continue telling stories until I beg him to stop."

So, many kinds of men came to him and told all their best stories. But however long they kept on talking, he never got bored. He always wanted to hear more of the story. He would urge the teller to continue, saying "Then what happened?" or "So? And then?" None of them could keep talking until he said "Stop!"

One day, a poor man came and said he wanted to try telling a story. He said, "As I tell, I want you to chime in, 'Yes, that's totally true.'"

The rich man said, "It sounds interesting. Very well, I will say, 'Yes, that's totally true' after every line of your story. All right, go ahead and start."

So the young man began:
Speak rhythmically, and encourage your listeners to stay in rhythm with you.
"You're a very rich man."

"Yes, that's totally true."
"The richest in three counties."
"Yes, that's totally true."
"I am just a poor man."
"Yes, that's totally true."

The rich man was enjoying this very much. And the other people, who had come to enjoy the storytelling, also liked this game and began chanting, "Yes, that's totally true" along with the rich man.

"My father was a poor man."
"Yes, that's totally true."
"But grandpa made some money."
"Yes, that's totally true."
"He saved a thousand *ryo*."
"Yes, that's totally true."
"He lent money to other people."
"Yes, that's totally true."
"Your grandpa came to borrow some."
"Yes, that's totally true."
"He borrowed three hundred."
"Yes, that's totally true."
"But before he paid the money back…"
"Yes, that's totally true."
"… he died … and left the debt to his grandchildren… …"

The rich man was surprised and shouted, "What are you talking about? My grandpa never borrowed money from your grandpa!"

But the other people were enjoying the story and wanted it to continue. They chanted,
"Yes, that's totally true."
So the poor man kept on talking.
"It's only right to pay a debt back."
"Yes, that's totally true."

"You should pay me with money."

"Yes, that's totally true."

"But I'd gladly take your daughter."

" — Stop! That's enough! Stop talking!" cried the rich man.

The poor man smiled and continued, "He said that I should stop."

"Yes, that's totally true."

"Did everybody hear him?"

"Yes, that's totally true."

"That means I win the contest."

"Yes, that's totally true."

"His daughter is my bride now."

"Yes, that's totally true."

"She's the best bride anywhere."

"Yes, that's totally true."

"So we will be very happy."

"Yes, that's totally true."

"And this story has a very happy ending!"

"Yes,… that's
totally…
true!"

"*Shyaan shyaan!* (This is the end of my story.)"

So the poor man married the rich man's daughter and lived happily ever after.

Shyaan shyaan!

Comments

This is a story where listeners enjoy joining in together with the storyteller. The listeners' part is "Yes, that's totally true." (In Japanese, *"Haa sono tori."*) Even if you don't instruct them, "Everybody, say this together," you will find that after you repeat it two or three times they will join in. But because this story has both ordinary text and rhythmical parts, I recommend that you practice the transitions.

This is a very traditional way to tell a story in Japan. When a teller says, "An old man went to the mountains to cut firewood," listeners chime in with *"Hun"* or *"Sorede? (And then?)"* If listeners respond rhythmically, the teller can tell rhythmically.

The person who told this story to me said, "We used to listen to grandma tell us stories while she was spinning and winding the threads on her hand-cranked spinning wheel. As she said 'Long time ago there were …' she would turn the wheel once. We listeners chimed in, '*Sorede? (And then?)*'

"'…a very old man and a very old woman…' She turned the wheel again. We said, 'And then?'

"When she turned the wheel very slowly, she told the story very slowly. And while we listeners chimed in at every turn, we would listen very intently."

The response differs in different parts of Japan. I have heard that in some places they say *"Otto"* or *"Sansuke."* At Shimohusa in Chiba Prefecture the listeners responded *"Hego-hego."*

Frog Cakes

Before you begin, put milk carton "frogs" into the box and wrap it with a carrying cloth.

You may need to explain to your audience what botamochi *are and how these bumpy brown snacks do look a bit like frogs (see Comment on the next page).*

Once upon a time there lived a stingy and ill-tempered old woman. She was so mean that she ate all the tastiest food herself without sharing it with her son's wife, but she let her daughter-in-law do all the hard work without any help.

One day when this greedy Grandma was going out for an errand, a neighbor visited her and gave her a box full of delicious *botamochi. She* loved *botamochi.*

But she had a problem. If she ate the *botamochi* now she would be late for the errand. If she left them behind, she worried that her daughter-in-law might eat them. She thought about what to do, and had an idea.

She untied the carrying cloth, lifted the lid a bit, and said something to the *botamochi.*

Do these motions, pretending to whisper something to the box contents.

But the son's wife passed by the room and, hearing her mother-in-law's voice through the thin wall, she stopped to listen.

She overheard the mother-in-law say to the box, "You *botamochi,* listen to me carefully. I am going out for an errand. If my son's wife opens this box, turn into *frogs.* Understand? Turn into frogs. But when I open the box, turn back into *botamochi.* All right? If my daughter-in-law opens the box, become frogs. But for me, become *botamochi."*

The old woman repeated this many times. She closed the lid, wrapped the box in the carrying cloth, put the box on the family altar

Do these motions as you tell the story.

and went out to do her errand. "Now I am going," she said.

The son's wife said "Bye, bye!" politely to her mother-in-law, but she was really angry. "Very well, if Grandma wants to change the *botamochi* into frogs, I will do that."

She ate all the *botamochi* in the box, and went to the rice field and caught a lot of frogs. She put the frogs into the box, tied it up, and returned it to the family altar.

Pretend to do these things.

After a while, the old woman came home. She went directly to the family altar. When she lifted the box she said, "Oh, this is heavy enough, all the *botamochi* are still inside. My daughter-in-law didn't find them. Now I have time to eat them all myself."

So she untied the carrying cloth. But when she peeked into the box, she was astonished to see a slimy face looking back at her.

Lift the lid a bit, but shut it in a hurry.

"What is this?" she wondered, but then she remembered what she had said to the box before she went out. "Oh, yes. I told you to become frogs. You did a good job. You are very clever. But this is not my son's wife, it's *me*, the Grandma. So you can turn back into *botamochi*."

Open the lid a bit again, and shut it fast.
She opened the box again, but all she saw was froggy faces. She closed the box.
Do it.

"This is not my son's wife. This is myself."
When she opened the box again, the frogs peeked out. She closed the box.
"This is not my son's wife! This is me — Grandma!"
As she repeatedly opened and closed the box,
Pretend to do as the story says.

a small frog jumped out.
"Hey, *botamochi!* Don't go away!" She caught the frog and put it back into the box. But another one jumped out of the box.
"Hey, you, *botamochi*. Don't escape!"
When she tried to put back one from this side, others came out from the other side.
The frogs, tired of being crowded in the small box, jumped out a few at a time. But the greedy Grandma, still thinking they were *botamochi*, cried out, "Don't hop! If you hop so hard, your sweet topping will fall off, and that's the best part!"
So saying, the old woman chased the frogs, but all the *botamochi* disappeared in the end, and the greedy Grandma didn't get any sweet cakes.

Let's see. Are there really frogs in this box?
*Open the lid and release
the prepared frogs.*

Comment

You can build up the tension and humor in this story when the mother-in-law comes home and scolds the frogs because they won't change back into sweet cakes. Repeat variations on her interaction with the frogs many times, making it as slapstick as the audience will enjoy.

I recommend practicing in advance with the box so that you can make the frogs jump out at the end of the story.

Note: When Fujita-san tells this story, she uses a *juubako*: a traditional Japanese lidded laquer or plastic box for carrying your lunch or for presenting food gifts. By bouncing it on her knees to rattle the lid, she can make children believe that there are really live frogs inside! At the end of the story, when she takes off the lid and releases the milk carton "frogs," the children shriek with surprise and delight.

Note about botamochi: *Botamochi* are a very popular snack in Japan. The rice center is covered with a fudgey brown topping made from mashed dark red-brown beans and sugar. When American listeners hear that the bumpy brown, oval cakes resemble our chocolate-covered coconut candy Easter eggs, it's easy for them to imagine that they look a bit like frogs....

How To:

Materials: rinsed, dried milk cartons (a half-pint makes 1 frog; quart makes 3 frogs or one box to hold 12-15 frogs) rubber bands
Tools: scissors, tape, stapler.

Frogs: Cut on heavy lines as shown.

Cut 1/2" notches into corners ABCD of each section as shown. Hook a rubber band into the cuts. (Store frog with band relaxed.)

To make the frog jump, flatten it so that the rubber band is stretched; release suddenly.

Box: Make bottom from one lengthwise half, using the carton bottom for one end and making the other end as show. Make top from the other half, fastening it on with tape or staples. Note slit to hold tab fastener.

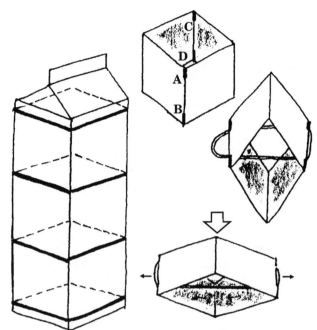

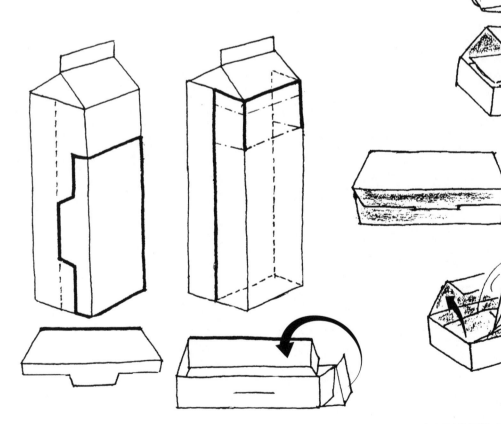

Boing!

Afterword

Children like stories. People say that children won't listen to stories these days because of television, but I don't think that's the problem. It's not that children won't listen, it's that fewer adults tell stories. I think children will always listen to stories with joy.

When I was a child, I listened to stories from the farmer who cultivated the field next door. When we saw a frog jump, he told me a story about how this frog came out of an old woman's *juubako*. When a dog piddled, he told a story about why dogs raise their hind leg. When a snake came out, he told a story about snakes. When flowers bloomed, he told a story about flowers. What joy that gave me! Stories start when people face each other. I wish to share that joy with children.

Now we have a lot of milk cartons or newspapers around us. I thought I could use such things to play with children. I thought, I want to tell stories with a milkbox puppet that looks like a frog, or a newspaper folded to look like a mountain. My opinion is that happy stories are important to help people face each other, and to develop the power of imagination.

A few years ago I met American storyteller Fran Stallings. I had the chance to play with American children, using milk carton puppets and dolls made from cotton gloves. I knew the children would enjoy playing with me, but I also thought it would be difficult for them to understand my stories. Yet to my surprise, in every school, children listened to my stories very eagerly. Before I told my stories (in Japanese), they heard outlines of the stories (in English) and I used one or two props. But American children listened to my Japanese stories very enthusiasticaly and enjoyed them very much.

I saw children listen carefully and enjoy the rhythm of the stories. I saw children laugh out loud when they felt the humor. Their active, expressive response was different from what I expect from Japanese children (who are somewhat more reserved), but it gave me the same good feelings.

The American schools that invited me to visit think that stories are important. And in those schools there are a lot of teachers who are also storytellers. So the children must be accustomed to hearing stories. The mood in those schools was very good.

When I talked with American teachers, many of them introduced themselves to me: "I am a teacher, and also a storyteller." At storytelling festivals, school teachers as well as librarians got together. There are a lot of colleges whose Department of Education requires a course in storytelling. In elementary school, there are storytelling classes. America is a very wide country and there are some differences between states. So I mustn't make a sweeping statement, but I had the impression that America is a country where people treasure the telling of stories. I found many books about how to tell stories, for example, *Story Times for Two Year Olds* (Judy Nichols, American Library Association, 1987), and books about how to tell to the upper years. When I read those books, I admired the fact that in this country there are so many people who try to tell stories. And there are a lot of interesting and easy books of stories that a beginner can tell. Fran-san taught me some of those stories, which Japanese children would enjoy.

In Japan I believe there are a lot of people who would like to tell stories. For such people I wrote this book. I enjoy telling stories, but preparing a book was not as much fun. I had a lot of help from my publisher, Ookura-san, who encouraged me, and from Kobayashi-san who cheerfully did the illustrations. And so this book was completed.

Please read this. And tell these stories.

— *Hiroko Fujita*

Profile of Hiroko Fujita

Hiroko Fujita was born in Tokyo in 1937. When World War II threatened, her father evacuated the family to the small rural town of Miharu in mountainous Fukushima Prefecture, where she grew up listening to old stories. She has told stories during her forty years as a teacher and counselor of Japanese kindergarten (3-5 years) children. Now she travels widely in Japan, telling stories at kindergartens, elementary schools, colleges, and libraries, and lecturing to adults about the educational value of sharing traditional stories.

And she has been invited by storyteller friends to visit America, where she has introduced old Japanese stories, nursery rhymes, and games at schools and libraries of many states in her annual spring tours. She has been a featured teller at the Texas Storytelling Festival and the St. Louis Festival at the Arch. She has presented workshops at American universities, libraries, and conferences nationwide.

Her published works in Japan include:

Old Stories of Fukushima told by Toshiko Endo a joint work with folklorist Kauo Yoshizawa (Tokyo: Isseisha Publishing Company, 1995)

Shittakaburi Collected essays by Hiroko Fujita (Tokyo: Taihou-sha Publishing Company, 1996)

Katare Yamanba Stories told by Hiroko Fujita, Volumes 1, 2, and 3 (Tokyo: Taihou-sha Publishing Company, 1996, 1997, 1998)

Ohanashi Obasan-no Dogu (Storytelling Auntie's Gadgets) Volumes 1 and 2 (Tokyo: Isseisha Publishing Company, 1996 and 1998)

— Fran Stallings

Postscript

I met Mrs. Fujita in Japan in the summer of 1993, and have had the honor of arranging annual spring tours of America for her since 1995. American children loved her storytelling. Their teachers and librarians clamored for instructions on how to make the toys and games that she used with the stories. When she published *Ohanashi Obasan-no Dogu* (literally, "Storytelling Auntie's Gadgets") in Japan in the summer of 1996, we realized that it was the answer to American storytellers' requests.

This was perhaps the first Japanese handbook for beginning tellers who work with young children. The informal, playful, family style of storytelling for children is called *obasan* (auntie) or *katari* (chatting, gossip, lie!) style. In Japan, there are formal guilds of professional storytellers, but they do not tell these types of stories and do not work in elementary schools. Storytelling for children has been granted little recognition. But the recent storytelling revival movement in Japan, and Fujita-san's work and publications, are helping to change that attitude.

I was delighted to find in this book several stories which Fujita-san heard from me. They are simple stories which I often use to train beginning tellers in America. Clearly Fujita-san felt that they would be helpful for Japanese beginners, too. In this translation they are coming home to America, along with her own traditional and original Japanese stories.

The Japanese publisher and illustrator kindly gave their permission to adapt this book for American readers. We have made small changes in some of the artwork to adapt it for reprinting here, and have substituted others of Fujita-san's stories for a few which we felt would not translate accessibly into English.

English translations were prepared with the generous assistance of Mrs. Satomi Obata and Mrs. Mitsuko Harada, who deserve the credit. I adapted the text into American storytelling style, and deserve the blame for any infelicitous phrases. I am indebted to the many American readers, particularly Beth DeGeer of the Bartlesville Public Library, who helped me evaluate and refine these versions for American children.

— *Fran Stallings*

Story Sources

Hiroko Fujita adapted, arranged, and retold the stories in this book from the following sources, with the help of countless children in Japan and America:

14	Which One Won?	Japanese traditional fingerplay
15	Mr. Brown & Mr. Black	American children's tradition
20	Ms. Fox	Japanese traditional game
22	A Mysterious House	original activity by Hiroko Fujita
24	Crab's Persimmons	traditional Japanese story
26	Squeak! Squeak! Squeak!	Japanese traditional fingerplay
29	I Wish Today Was My Birthday!	original activity by Hiroko Fujita
32	Doggie Policeman	Japanese children's song
34	What Kind of Egg is This?	Japanese traditional origami
36	My Mommy Is Gone	original story by Hiroko Fujita
38	Turkey Lake	American children's tradition *
42	Rain Hat	American children's tradition *
48	The Old Coat	American story *
50	One is Missing!	traditional Japanese game
52	Mountain Climbing	original story by Hiroko Fujita
56	Burglar's Hideout	original story by Hiroko Fujita
60	Dandelion	original story by Hiroko Fujita
62	The Only Thing I Am Afraid Of Is	original story by Hiroko Fujita
64	Cluck Cluck Hen	traditional Japanese children's song
67	Hanky Stories	Japanese traditional origami
70	A Pile of Stuff	traditional Japanese story
74	Wide-Mouth Frog	traditional American story *
76	Mouse's Marriage	traditional Japanese story
78	I Want...	traditional Japanese story
80	That's Totally True	traditional Japanese story
83	Frog Cakes	traditional Japanese story

*Hiroko Fujita first heard these from Fran Stallings. Fran learned "Rain Hat" and "The Old Coat" from Nancy Schimmel.

In the American edition, "Crab's Persimmons" and "I Wish Today Was My Birthday" replace stories that did not cross the culture gap.

Story Notes and Suggested Applications

GENERAL NOTES ON MATERIALS

Origami: You don't need imported origami paper, but you do need perfect squares. You can recycle office paper and advertising supplements (whose colored inks don't rub off as readily as black newsprint). Try teaching children the rules for making a perfect square: parallel sides, all sides of equal length.

Cotton gloves: Lightweight cotton knit gloves are more comfortable and versatile than canvas work gloves or wooly winter gloves. In Japan, where such gloves are very popular for even the lightest work, they are cheap and come in wonderful colors. Here, look for thin knit gardening gloves, cotton glove liners, and cotton "roping gloves."

THE STORIES

Which Side Won? (page 14)

Sometimes even young children giggle nervously at the middle finger. They don't know what it means, but they may have seen older children gesture with rude intent. The gesture is culturally specific, not universal. In our experience, if you calmly continue the story indicating that *you* mean it to stand for Big Brother, children have no trouble with it.

Mr. Brown and Mr. Black (page 15)

This is an excellent story for bilingual telling or for working entirely in second languages. Even if every word is unfamiliar, listeners can follow the story from your gestures. They readily learn to mimic the actions, and then the words. They love to perform it! Try introducing new vocabulary by telling it in the familiar language with just a few key words in the second tongue; then add more and more.

Ms. Fox (page 20)

New Englanders remember playing a similar childhood game featuring a wolf in place of the fox! Showing the game with gloves allows everyone to participate in the chant without classroom mayhem. Such glove play can also be used to teach new games which the children can then play outdoors. Try "Simon Says," "Red Light, Green Light," and other games you remember.

A Mysterious House (page 22)

You can keep this as a puzzle to bemuse children in between stories, or teach older children to do the trick for younger ones. Any four animal faces can be used. Try teaching children the animals' names in another language. (See the note on "I Wish Today Was My Birthday" explaining why these four animals are special in Japan.)

Crab's Persimmons (page 24)

This traditional tale lets children laugh at the frustration of a bully. The little book is fun to make for other stories, whose nouns and verbs help with second language learning.

Squeak! Squeak! Squeak! (page 26)

Try using these mice to teach counting in other languages, or with other nursery songs about counting. When Japanese mice squeak, they say, *"Chu chu chu!"*

I Wish Today Was My Birthday (page 29)

There is a nursery song about these four animals which helps Japanese children learn to distinguish syllables, which is important since they initially learn to read and write with a phonetic syllabary (not an alphabet). The song goes *"Kobuta* (piglet), *Tanuki* (Raccoon), *Kitsune* (Fox), *Neko* (Cat)" and back to *"Kobuta,"* etc. Notice how the last syllable of each name is the first syllable of the next! Try finding a series of English words whose syllables chain together like this.

Doggie Policeman (page 32)

This story is a funny way to help young children remember the information they must know in case they become lost. The puppets can also help very young children practice our culture's head-shaking gestures for yes and no.

What Kind of Egg Is This? (page 34)

Older children are fascinated by this hexaflexagon. The first step teaches a handy way to measure 60 degrees (geometry).

Try using this to teach vocabulary words for geometrical terms and folding steps; various types of egg, juvenile, and mature animal.

My Mommy Is Gone (page 36)

The Japanese animal I am calling "Raccoon" is actually *tanuki*, a member of the dog family (sometimes translated as "badger," but it's not that either). The woods-dwelling *tanuki* has a fox-like body and a broad, masked face and ringed tail. He plays a prominent role in Japanese folktales as a trickster (like Coyote in America) and a shape-changer. Traditional lore says that *Tanuki* has a potbelly which he can beat like a drum, especially under the full moon: "Pon poko pon poko!"

Monkeys *(Saru)* also live wild in the mountains of many parts of Japan. Try using other animals to tell this story.

Turkey Lake (page 38)

Older children enjoy learning to tell a story while drawing a surprise. This one is good to teach just before Thanksgiving vacation, when they can show it off to relatives. Often family members will then be reminded of one they learned long ago!

Try making up a new story as you draw a stylized picture.

Rain Hat (page 42)

Steps 5-8 (hose, ladder) were added to this American story by Hiroko Fujita. They are fun and dramatic, but require extra paper, tape, and scissors. Beginners might start with just the original story, which uses and reuses a single sheet of newsprint and requires no tools.

The "V" sign made by the child at the end of the story is used in Japan like our thumb-and-finger-together sign to mean "Fine!" or "I did it!" I have also seen Japanese children use this sign when photos are being taken: instead of saying "cheese," they say "peace" and hold up two fingers.

The Old Coat (page 48)

This story can help teach vocabulary for the different garments the tailor made. Try inventing a new story following the pattern: something big wears out (crashes, breaks down) but there's enough left to make something a little smaller, which eventually wears out, et cetera. You can stay with one character, or bring new people into the story at each step.

One is Missing! (page 50)

This is another good story for practicing counting words and animal sounds. (Japanese pigs say *"Bu bu bu!"*) For small children, use only five animals. Try using different animal toys, origami, or cut-outs

Mountain Climbing (page 52)

Even tough alternative high school students enjoyed learning this story to retell for young children. It brought back good memories of learning these paper-folds, and they were eager to share. Compare this story with "Rain Hat" (page 42). Try making up new stories using these and other newspaper shapes.

Burglar's Hideout (page 56)

This slight-of-hand novelty is fun between stories, and older children enjoy learning to mystify their siblings. If you are uncomfortable with the burglar protagonist, try the Santa variation or invent one where someone else needs a hideout and a disguise.

Dandelion (page 60)

This is an example of how a playful story can be invented on the spot! It is also useful for teaching animal names and noises. See the story's comment for some Japanese animal sounds. Try using different animal toys or pictures.

The Only Thing I Am Afraid Of Is — (page 62)

Listeners of all ages enjoy the story's circularity. We're all afraid of something. Instead of stick puppets, try using plain double-sided pictures or standing cards (as in "A Pile of Stuff" page 70).

Cluck Cluck Hen (page 64)

This story helps young children practice the chicken life cycle and counting to 21. The slight-of-hand takes practice! Try making up new stories with the hen and her chicks.

Hanky Stories (page 67)

Since you can also use paper tissues or napkins, this story is very handy while waiting in a restaurant! After children learn these, they can ask older folks if they remember some other handkerchief shapes and try making up new stories with them.

Note: these are the original Japanese illustrations, and they are typical in dress and facial features. Notice the western clothing on everyone except Grandma. But Mama Hanky wears slippers: Japanese folks always leave their street shoes at the door.

A Pile of Stuff (page 70)

This tale's formulaic plot, with cause and effect connections between steps, is very easy for beginners to learn. Try using it in a unit about weather and the environment to introduce meteorologists' explanations of rain and wind.

Wide-Mouth Frog (page 74)

Fujita-san learned this American tale from Fran, who often uses it to help beginners practice tandem telling. After telling the story solo, Fran demonstrates with a volunteer how one person can speak for the little frog, while the other can take all the other roles. Then pairs of students can practice the story together. A milkbox frog puppet (made as in "Doggie Policeman" page 32) is handy for shy beginners. Try this tandem format with other tales that have continuing characters, like "A Pile of Stuff" (page 70: the questioning children) and "Mouse's Marriage" (page 76: the parents).

Mouse's Marriage (page 76)

Since Japanese mice say "chu" (squeak), the bride and groom's names might be translated "Little Squeak" and "Squeaker."
This story motif, "Strongest of All," occurs worldwide in folktales. The plots are usually circular and easy for beginners to remember. Try using this and similar tales for second language vocabulary.

I Want ... (page 78)

We found that American children understand and enjoy this story even though it hinges on a second-language pun. (The opening explanation is important.) Try thinking of pairs of English words which sound the same but have different meanings (homophones). If there isn't already a pun story about them, try making one up! Do you know puns in any other language?

That's Totally True (page 80)

Many cultures tell about a storytelling contest (or a liar's contest) which will be won when someone says "Stop!" or "I don't believe that!" The protagonist tells a tricky story which the judge doesn't want others to hear. Several variants are known from Japan. This particular tale, however, seems to be unique to Fukushima Prefecture where Fujita-san learned it in childhood. Older students and adults enjoy chanting the rhythmic refrain in Japanese: "*Haa, sono tori!*"

Frog Cakes (page 83)

This folktale, whose motifs are known throughout Japan, can be told effectively without any props. However, the cascade of frogs leaping from the box at the end of the story provides a wonderful grand finale for any storytelling program.

When the old woman put the box on the family altar, she was following an ancient custom in presenting any new thing to the ancestors before using/eating it herself. If this is confusing to your listeners, just say she put it up on the "shelf."

Children love to make frogs from their lunch milkboxes and invent games and contests using them. Middle school students actually drank milk instead of pop! Try taping many frogs together at the unclipped ends to make a leaping snake.

During Fujita-san's childhood there were no cardboard milkboxes, but children made the frogs from thin wooden wafers on which certain delicatessen treats were sold. Poor country children made many kinds of toys from adults' trash and natural objects (pebbles, pine needles, wild flowers, and leaves). Interestingly, affluent American children are fascinated by the notion of making their own toys out of found materials: it's not just recycling, it's independence.